JESUS AS A PATTERN

JESUS AS A PATTERN

For Every Soul on Earth

By Edgar Cayce

ARE
PRESS

ASSOCIATION FOR
RESEARCH AND
ENLIGHTENMENT

A.R.E. Press • Virginia Beach • Virginia

A.R.E. Press
215 67th Street
Virginia Beach, VA 23451-2061

ISBN-13: 978-0-87604-533-6 (trade pbk.)

Editor's Note
All of Edgar Cayce's discourses are now available on CD-ROM from A.R.E. Press at AREBookstore.com or 800-333-4499.

Cover design by Richard Boyle

Contents

Foreword
Who Was Edgar Cayce?

Edgar Cayce (1877–1945) has been called "the Sleeping Prophet," "the father of Holistic medicine," "the miracle man of Virginia Beach," and "the most documented psychic of all time." For forty-three years of his adult life, he had the ability to put himself into some kind of self-induced sleep state by lying down on a couch, closing his eyes, and folding his hands over his stomach. This state of relaxation and meditation enabled him to place his mind in contact with all time and space and to respond to any question he was asked. His responses came to be called "readings" and contain insights so valuable that, even to this day, Cayce's work is known throughout the world. Hundreds of books have explored his amazing psychic gift, and the entire range of Cayce material is accessed by tens of thousands of people daily via the Internet.

Although the vast majority of the Cayce material deals with health and every manner of illness, countless topics were explored by Cayce's psychic talent: dreams, philosophy, intuition, business advice, the Bible, education, child rearing, ancient civilizations, personal spirituality, improving human relationships, and much more. In fact, during Cayce's lifetime he discussed an amazing ten thousand different subjects!

The Cayce legacy presents a body of information so valuable that

Edgar Cayce himself might have hesitated to predict its impact on contemporary society. Who could have known that eventually, terms such as *meditation, auras, spiritual growth, reincarnation,* and *holism* would become household words to millions? Edgar Cayce's A.R.E. (the Association for Research and Enlightenment, Inc.) has grown from its humble beginnings to an association with Edgar Cayce Centers in countries around the world. Today the Cayce organizations consist of hundreds of educational activities and outreach programs, children's camps, a multi-million-dollar publishing company, membership benefits and services, volunteer contacts and programs worldwide, massage and health services, prison and prayer outreach programs, conferences and workshops, and affiliated schools (Atlantic University and the Cayce/Reilly School of Massotherapy).

Edgar Cayce was born and reared on a farm near Hopkinsville, Kentucky. He had a normal childhood in many respects. However, he could see the glowing energy patterns that surround individuals. At a very early age he also told his parents that he could see and talk with his grandfather—who was deceased. Later, he developed the ability to sleep on his schoolbooks and retain a photographic memory of their entire contents.

As the years passed, he met and fell in love with Gertrude Evans, who would become his wife. Shortly thereafter, he developed a paralysis of the vocal cords and could scarcely speak above a whisper. Everything was tried, but no physician was able to locate a cause. The laryngitis persisted for months. As a last resort, hypnosis was tried. Cayce put himself to sleep and was asked by a specialist to describe the problem. While asleep, he spoke normally, diagnosing the ailment and prescribing a simple treatment. After the recommendations were followed, Edgar Cayce could speak normally for the first time in almost a year! The date was March 31, 1901—that was the first reading.

When it was discovered what had happened, many others began to want help. It was soon learned that Edgar Cayce could put himself into this unconscious state and give readings for anyone—regardless of where he or she was. If the advice was followed, the individual got well. Newspapers throughout the country carried articles about his work, but it wasn't really until Gertrude was stricken with tuberculosis that the readings were brought home to him. Even with medical treatments, she continued to grow worse and was not expected to live. Finally, the doctors said there was nothing more they could do. A reading was given and recommended osteopathy, inhalants, enemas, dietary changes, and prescription medication. The advice was followed and Gertrude returned to perfectly normal health! For decades, the Cayce readings have stood the test of time, research, and extensive study. Further details of Cayce's life and work are explored in such classic books as *There Is a River* (1942) by Thomas Sugrue, *The Sleeping Prophet* (1967) by Jess Stearn, *Many Mansions* (1950) by Gina Cerminara, and *Edgar Cayce: An American Prophet* (2000) by Sidney Kirkpatrick.

Throughout his life, Edgar Cayce claimed no special abilities, nor did he ever consider himself to be some kind of twentieth-century prophet. The readings never offered a set of beliefs that had to be embraced but instead focused on the fact that each person should test in his or her own life the principles presented. Though Cayce himself was a Christian and read the Bible from cover to cover for every year of his life, his work was one that stressed the importance of comparative study among belief systems all over the world. The underlying principle of the readings is the oneness of all life, a tolerance for all people, and a compassion and understanding for every major religion in the world.

An Overview of Edgar Cayce on
Jesus as a Pattern

Over a three-year period, Jesus the Nazarene amassed a group of followers who would eventually provide for one of the greatest religious transformations the world would ever know. These people from all walks and stations of life followed after Him because of His promises, the allure of His presence, and the impact of His ministry. Perhaps, more than anything else, it was Jesus' miracles of healing that first attracted so many to Him. His fame spread throughout the Holy Land and, almost as quickly, disagreements arose as to just "Who was this man?" Consensus on that one question has eluded much of humankind for the last two thousand years.

Throughout history, the perspectives people have had on the life and teachings of Jesus have been varied, oftentimes even at odds. Some individuals involved in "new age philosophies" or comparative religious studies have sometimes decided that Jesus was "just a teacher." Others have decided to disregard Him altogether. Was He only a prophet? Members of non-Christian faiths may have ignored His life and ministry. Others may have said, "Well, Christians have been cruel to me, and therefore I'm not interested in Jesus." Was He a man who committed blasphemy by thinking Himself God? Even among those who call themselves Christian, there is no complete agreement about His divinity. Disagreements over the meaning of His life and ministry have resulted in dozens of denominational factions, charges of heresy or breaking away from the faith, and countless wars. Was He the only son of God? Was He a God who became man or always God?

The perspective on Jesus in the Edgar Cayce material is unique in that it presents Jesus' life as having meaning for *every* soul in the earth, not simply for those who call themselves Christian. In fact, the readings state that Jesus was a pattern for every soul in the earth—somehow the way in which Jesus manifested the full awareness of the spirit in the earth is a pattern of behavior for each and every soul. With this in mind, Cayce called Jesus our "Elder brother"—a soul who came to show each one of us the way back to our spiritual Source by perfectly manifesting the laws of the Creator. Jesus' life of service provides an example for all of humankind, and from Cayce's perspective, each individual will ultimately be challenged to manifest that same pattern in his or her life. One of the readings describes it in this manner: "For the Master, Jesus, even the Christ, is the pattern for every man in the earth, whether he be Gentile or Jew, Parthenian or Greek. For all have the pattern, whether they call on that name or not . . . " (3528-1)

Elsewhere, Cayce suggested that this pattern of perfection could be called the Christ Consciousness, which was described as the "awareness within each soul, imprinted in pattern on the mind and waiting to be awakened by the will, of the soul's oneness with God." (5749-14) Regardless of an individual's religious or personal beliefs, this Christ pattern exists in potential upon the very fiber of her or his being. It is that unique portion of each individual that remains in perfect accord with the Creator and is simply waiting to find expression in the earth.

From Cayce's perspective, seeing Jesus as a pattern for life is helpful in the same way that an older sibling can sometimes provide insight and counsel into life's difficulties because he or she went through them first. Thus, Jesus is not interested in religious conversion, denominationalism, or even mighty, personal accomplishments. Instead, He is simply interested in how we love one another and how well we apply our love for God in the earth. This same counsel was given to Thomas Sugrue, author of Cayce's biography *There Is a River*, when he was told the ultimate lesson that could be learned from Jesus as the pattern:

What *will* ye do with this man thy elder brother, thy Christ, who—that thy Destiny might be sure in Him—has shown thee the more excellent way. Not in mighty deeds of valor, not in the exaltation of thy knowledge or thy power; but in the gentleness of the things of the spirit: Love, kindness, longsuffering, patience; these thy brother hath shown thee that thou, applying them in thy associations with thy fellow man day by day, here a little, there a little, may become one with Him as He has *destined* that thou shouldst be! Wilt thou separate thyself? For there be nothing . . . that may separate thee from the love of thy God, of thy brother, save thine own self!   **849–11**

For years, individuals from every background and religious tradition have found the Edgar Cayce information on Jesus extremely helpful in dealing with challenges as well as their own attitudes and emotions in daily life. This book of excerpts from the Cayce readings has been compiled to provide an understanding of Jesus the pattern as well as to explore some of the advice given to individuals who had readings and were told that the life of Jesus would be instructive for them personally. With this in mind, it may be read for insights into the readings' approach to Jesus or even as a daily devotional. This is the Jesus—Elder brother, wayshower, pattern for all of humankind—that is found in the Edgar Cayce readings.

Kevin J. Todeschi
Executive Director & CEO
Edgar Cayce's A.R.E. / Atlantic University

1

●

Understanding Relationships, with Jesus as the Pattern

[Background: Housewife, Protestant. This was a joint reading for her husband (1467) and herself in regard to their marriage and future; they were having many problems. Later, they worked these out and had a harmonious relationship; their marriage became an inspiration to others.]

Reading 263–18

GC: You will have before you the entities present in this room, [263], born April 16, 1911, near Murfreesboro, N.C., and [1467], born January 22, 1905, in Norfolk, Va.; also the information which has been given them through this channel. In the light of what has been given, what have they to work out together in the immediate future or in this experience? You will answer the questions they each have submitted, concerning their work; relationships to one another, in the home, outside of the home and with others. You will give such counsel as will help them to carry on and understand their duty, that there be more love and better understanding as to their relation to each other:

EC: Yes, we have the entities here, [263], [1467]; together with the information indicated through these channels as to their experiences in the earth, their relationships one to another.

In giving advice or counsel, it would be well that each analyze the information that has been indicated for each—their faults and failures *and* their virtues; and that each not attempt to find their differences but rather that upon which each *can* agree.

There *are* agreements in some directions. There are differences in many; yet, as is understood from the experiences of each, as well as the information indicated, it is *not* by chance that there is this union of activities in the present; but if each will accept same it is an opportunity through which each may be the gainer in the soul, mental, as well as material development.

If they each reject the opportunity—*if* they *each* reject the opportunity—it becomes sin, and *must* eventually be met.

Then, there is *every* reason for the *attempt*, at least, for each to meet these differences, and so little—save self, and selfishness, that prevents the attempt to at least meet the problems in the present.

There are those activities—as will be seen from an analysis of the activities in the earth—in which many differences arise, and many of the reasons materially why varied ideas are given expression to. Yet these should be such, in activity, as not to be magnified but minimized.

They each have their faults, they each have their virtues—as is shown. There must be *some* common ground for the reasoning.

As each understands—that which prompts the activity, in any individual, arises from a spiritual attitude, or of the spirit.

Let each then ask within self: With what spirit do I make this or that assertion? *Whose* kingdom, *Whose* judgment is being maintained by the attitudes I hold? Creative Energies, Creative Force or Power, or that which is destructive? That which is creative, or that which divides?

To be sure, when individuals attempt to look back upon faults or failures of one another, or to find condemning attitudes towards one another, these may bring remorse, quick judgment, defiance—as it does with each here.

Yet, as He gave—he that looketh back, he that hath once put his hand to the plow—meaning he that has determined to do the right, with the help of the faith in the Creative Force or God—he that has once set self in the direction of seeking to do the right, and *then* turns back—his estate, his condition becomes worse than ever.

Not in self may there be the interpreting of the problems. The *activi-*

ties must be in self. But ye each have an ideal—not ideas alone, but an ideal.

Study, then, to show thyself approved unto that ideal. Not merely because of what others may think, or because it is law, or because of that as may be said or thought, but because *self* desires to meet the problems—here—now!

And these will bring harmony, these will bring understanding; if there is the determination on the part of each to give and take.

It is not that either shall demand this or that of the other, but *demand of self that ye measure up to that the other would have you be—in the Christ!*

Ready for questions.

(Q) Why are we so uncomfortable with one another?

(A) They each have made up their mind they don't care and they don't like to be together; yet if they will analyze—together—those problems of each that have existed, and try—*try*—to meet them on a common basis, the situation will be understood and the uncomfortableness will be erased. Pray over it. Don't—*don't*—attempt to do the analyzing without taking it to Him!

(Q) How can we feel more married?

(A) By making the purposes of each as one.

(Q) Why is it so hard for us to agree on anything?

(A) Each looks for the differences, rather than that on which ye *can* agree!

(Q) Should we plan some specific hobby or recreation together, periodically? If so, what?

(A) This would be a very, *very* good start. Where the planning of recreation, of activity, of thought or study, or interest, is separate, ye grow apart. Where the interest may be together—whether in a hobby, in a recreation, in a study, in a visitation, in an association—ye grow in purpose as one.

The *law is, not* that ye may go one this way and the other that, and then your ideas and purposes be one; but where the treasure is, there may the heart be also, there may the activity be united.

(Q) When [1467] spends his time off with his son, should [263] occasionally go with him?

(A) This depends rather upon the son. While there should be interests alike, interests together—that there is a difference of opinions in such, it may depend more upon what *has* been said by others. But this, too, *can* be altered for good of all. It would be well to be undertaken, but once begun *don't* let it break the purposes!

(*Q*) *How should she conduct herself so as to produce harmony between the three?*

(A) In the same manner as ye ask, in the same manner ye desire that [1467] show toward thine own. These must be as a unison. Thy purposes, thy activities should be in the same accord as that deference, that judgment [1467] has shown, does show, toward thine own. This should be in keeping with the principles that have been set forth—seek *where ye may be of one purpose! Minimize the faults, magnify the virtues!*

(*Q*) *Do we live in the right environment?*

(A) *This* can only be answered within self. For, if there is the determination on the part of either that the environment or association is to be used as the *excuse*, then *nowhere* would be the right environment.

(*Q*) *Should* [1467] *continue to work with . . . Stores, Inc., or make a change?*

(A) We would not, through this particular period, make a change.

(*Q*) *Should he make more effort to collect the back and overtime pay due him and others at . . . Stores, Inc.? If so, how?*

(A) Through those channels of having the investigation by the Interstate Commerce Board.

(*Q*) *Should* [263] *continue to do Red Cross nursing?*

(A) If this is in agreement with those purposes that are determined by each, as to what the activities are to be, well and good. If it is not, or if it gives the expression of "I don't care," then better change!

(*Q*) *Please give a spiritual message specifically for* [263], *that will help her meet and overcome this period of strife.*

(A) Thy differences, thy hardships, thy crosses, are not peculiar to thyself alone; though ye oft think they are! There are as many crosses in the experience of [1467] as in self. Consider all phases of his experience, of thy experience. Study not as to what [1467] should do for thee, or as to how he should treat thee, but as to how Ye may so act, so speak, so be as to make that experience which will enable [1467] to better fulfil that he desires to do and be.

Thus it requires that just as much of such consideration be given thee by [1467] in that same attitude; not what he alone desires to do. But considering thy hardships, thy problems, he—too—striving to do and be that which will make thy purposes, thy aims—as agreed between selves—as to what ye hope to accomplish—more in accord with spiritual ideals.

There are many that ye influence day by day—not only in thine own home, but in thine acquaintance, among thy friends, among thy acquaintanceship, among even thy well-wishers and those that don't give a damn!

Then, so live, so act, one toward the other, as to make this experience—here and now—worth while! Not merely because of what others would say, not merely because it would please anyone, but thy Lord!

So live, then, that each activity is to the *glory* of God and to the *honor* of thy conscience!

(Q) *Please give a spiritual message specifically for [1467] that will help him meet and overcome this period of strife.*

(A) These are one. For, if there is the determination within self that "I won't agree to anything save my way," this is of little value. But if ye really seek, know that as given—all thy associations to the glory of thy hope in God, as manifested in Jesus, who found fault with none but forgave every one.

We are through for the present.

[Background: Housewife, Protestant. This was a joint reading for her husband (1650) and herself in regard to their marital problems. The couple were told that they had a number of things to work out between them; however, within a few years, they had divorced.]

Reading 1523–6

GC: You will have before you the entities present in this room, [1523], born December 2, 1908 in Oceana, Va., and [1650], born December 13, 1900; also the information which has been given them through this channel. In the light of what has been given, what have they to work out individually or together, in the immediate future or in this experience? You will answer the questions they each have submitted, as I ask them:

EC: Yes—we have the records of the entities here; [1650] and [1523].

In analyzing the experiences of these entities, it is well that there be given that premise from which such might be or is reasoned; that there may be an answering to each from within.

For unless that as may be given answers to something within, it can be of little help or value to either of these.

Know that each enters the experience into materialization for a purpose. That purpose is that each soul may be aware of its relationship to the Creative Forces—or God. Know that each enters with those activities in which each has lived and manifested, as a part of its natures, as a part of its *mental* environs.

Also know that the meeting, the association, the activity in the material experience in the present is *not* of chance but a purposeful experience for each; and that each may be a helpmeet one to the other in attaining and gaining such an understanding of the purposes for that meeting, that association, as to *attain* the correct concept of the *purpose* of their incoming or entrance into this material experience.

Know that this has not been completed in the present, and thus is to be *met in each!*

Then why not now?

It is a practical, it is a purposeful experience—for each.

For the associations in the past experience in the lands about the present environs, or a portion of the same land and those environs about the Dearborn land, are those problems that form the present disturbance in the mental selves.

Do not then justify *self* by condemning one another! Justify self rather by living, being that which will be a constructive experience in the life of *one another!*

For that is the *innate*, that is the real desire, that is the real purpose in each; else there would not have been that attraction one for the other.

For, have ye either of you analyzed what real love is?

It vaunteth not itself; it thinketh no evil; it endureth *all* things!

And this *is* the purpose, this *is* the basis for that attraction one to another.

If material things then are allowed to become barriers, in the manners of expressing this influence, then the condemning of either by the other is condemnation upon *self*—and must be *met* in self!

Study then to show thyself approved unto *God!* Be forgiving as ye would be forgiven. Remember that it is a partnership; not all to be given nor all to be taken by one. But do not *condemn* either, ever!

Let thy ideals be rather as is shown in *Him*, who patterned His experience in the earth among men in such a manner as to answer *every* question of conduct, of morality, of associations in *any* way and manner!

Then when ye are, either of thee in turmoil—*not* one shall do *all* the praying, nor all the "cussing"; but *together—ask!* and He will give—as He has promised—that assurance of peace, of harmony, that can *only* come from a coordinated, cooperative effort on the part of souls that seek to be the channels through which His love, His glory may be manifested in the earth! . . .

(Q) *Should [1650] or [1523] change their names? If so, what names would be suggested?*

(A) They each are significant of that they have to meet in each other. *Hold* that thou hast!

Let this be rather the determination of each:

I will keep myself in such an attitude, mentally and physically, that—cooperating with the other—I will give the greater manifestation of love and truth and virtue and understanding, in my daily life; that others may take courage also.

[Background: Housewife, Quaker. This was a physical, mental, and spiritual reading. Later, in a life reading, she was told that her best field of service was in spreading the light of truth, by practicing and telling it. She asked about several projects and, in each case, was told to examine her purposes and ideals—whether they were of the Christ or of self.]

Reading 1620–1

Then, wherein does the mind function? To use that thou hast in hand! What need is there for a better body, save to serve thy fellow man the better? For he that is the greatest among you is the servant of all. This is not only referring to those who teach, to those who minister, to those who wait on this, that or the other influence, but to each and every soul—and to every phase of the soul's activity in a material world!

Then, as to body and to mind both—purify same, cleanse same in the light of those things that He has given, for He is the way, He is the light.

Practice then in thy daily experience, and thy associations with thy fellow man, charity to all, love to all; finding fault with none; being patient with all, showing brotherly love and brotherly kindness. Against these there *is* no law! And ye who have put on and as ye put on these, by the application of them in thy dealings with thy fellow man, ye become free of the laws that are of body or of mind; for ye are then conscious of being one *with* the Creative Forces that bring into the experience and consciousness of all the love of the Father for the children of men.

And it is only as ye deal with thy fellowman that ye show forth His love. For as ye do it unto the least of these, thy brethren, ye do it unto thy Maker.

[Background: Bookkeeper, Protestant. She sought guidance regarding home relations and her alcoholic husband. She also sought advice for physical, mental, and spiritual development of all concerned.]

Reading 845-4

True, an individual, a soul, must become less and less of self—or thoughts of self; yet when those activities of others in *relationships* to the mental, the spiritual, the *soul* developments, are such that the own soul development an own soul expression becomes in jeopardy, then—as He hath given, "I came not to bring peace but a sword. I came to give peace, not as the world counts peace," but as that which makes for those experiences wherein the soul, the entity, is to *fulfill* those purposes, those activities, for which it—the soul-entity—came into being.

And when those relationships about same have been and are such that those conditions arise wherein there is the lack of harmonious effects that are possible, then as He hath given, put at naught those experiences, those influences. Let them be rather as they were not.

If there arises in the experience of self that which would become continuous as those upon which the entity would look back, in which the entity would think and think and worry, then continue—for the end is not yet.

But when there have been all of those experiences, all of those attempts, and there is still *naught*, then the jeopardy of self, of self-expression, of self-activity, as related with Creative Forces becomes as He hath given a division.

In the physical forces of the body there needs be *rest*, there needs be relief from *physical, mental* anxieties. For these continue in the present to make for that influence wherein the very vitality, the very life existence is being put into that position of where there is the rebellion between the spiritual, the mental, the material and the mental; and these make for such physical anxieties between the material forces and the soul forces that they rebel one with another.

Hence there come those injunctions as of old, "There is today set before thee good and evil, life and death—choose thou."

For He, thy example, thy mediator—yea, thy mentor is life, the father of life, the giver of peace, the giver of harmony.

These then are as conditions in all the relationships, in the home, in the associations, in the domestic relations, in the activities. Whatever thy choice is, let these be ever with an eye single to service to that living influence of being a better, a greater channel of blessings to someone.

Not of self-choosing an easier way; not of self attempting to escape that as is necessary for thine own understanding, thine own soul development; but rather ever, "Thy will, O Lord, be done in and through me—Use me as Thou seest I have need of, that I may be a living example of thy love, of thy guidance in this material experience."

[Background: Widow, podiatrist, Christian. This was a joint reading with (707) regarding their upcoming marriage and healing work together, connections in past incarnations, and spiritual and mental guidance. They married the next day and had a very happy union.]

Reading 688-4

EC: Yes, we have the entities here, [688] and [707]; their associations, their activities through the experiences in the earth; their relationships in the present that, as we find, may be made—by their associations and activities—as a unison of purpose in such measures, in such manners as to become those influences, those forces for helpful experience to themselves and as an aid, as a blessing to others . . .

First, as in making then the application of same, we see that in their
development they have ideas individually; yet basically, centrally, their
ideals are one. As they each make their individual application of that
which motivates their influences in giving expression of these, patience,
persistence, consistency must be the basic influence, the basic truth, the
basic force that would make for that which would make or bring into
the experience of each, not what is ordinarily termed as development
"down the road of life together" but rather *up* the road, back to those
influences and imports towards the light.

Each giving, each taking; each realizing the whole necessity of their
making their expressions to be compatible with the purposes not of
self, not of self–glorification, not for self–indulgences, not for self–ag-
grandizements that they may be in any instance just well–spoken of by
others; but rather that the glory of the Lord, that the purposes which
have prompted the heart of each, may be manifested. And this means
first *tolerance* as one to another.

There is the realization in the *experiences* materially of each of the
shortcomings here and there. Yet *self* must be effaced as to any conditions that make for fear, that would unseat the principles within self.

How, then, is asked, can these be made more and more compatible in
their activities? Realizing the short–comings in each, how may they be
made as a union of purposes in such measures, in such manners that
they *become* then as one in their expression?

Show forth in thine *own* life, each as one preferring the other! How
hath He given? Thou shalt love the Lord thy God with all thy heart, thy
mind, thy soul, thy body; and thy neighbor, thy brother, as thyself.

In what manner may these souls, as one, find then expression in
bringing to those that are troubled in body, in mind?

They have their individual methods or manners of approach. To one
it is *innate* and finds expression by the laying on of hands, by holding
within self the abilities for the replenishing, the quickening of life itself
in the very activity; by the *means* of subjugation of those influences in
and about others. To the other it is an activative force; one reaching or
gaining its access through its *spiritual* development and spiritual import,
yet means not only by implication but by the applying of that which

may be termed as the use of energies in nature itself—that is the handmaid to every individual that not only dedicates itself but that makes application within its experience of the glories that the Lord hath poured into the minds and hearts of the children of men, that they may know!

Then unifying these, let both in their own method, in their own manner apply same; yet knowing deep within self that the *source* of power, the *source* of might, the *source* of grace, the *source* of mercy, the *source* of life, the *source* of health comes only from the *living* God!

And each then becomes as a stay one for the other; becoming as a prop, as a brace, as a helpmeet.

In these manners, through the effacing of self, these influences may be wrought in such manners that many, *many* will call them blessed, *many* will give the glory to God; not to them, not to their efforts, but that they make themselves channels through which the glory and the might and the power of the Lord may be made manifest!

Not that turmoils, not that strifes oft, not that disappointment in the activities of men and of individuals here and there will not make for hardships. But *even then*, if their purposes are only that they may—as one, effacing self—show forth the glory of *God*, they may become—through such experiences—a strengthening influence one to another.

Through that which has been given each in their experiences in the earth is shown how they have had this or that in their experiences which has created, has builded the present conflicting influences. *Meet them!* In what? He, thy King, thy Lord; yea, thy Brother hath *shown* thee the way! "I am the way; I am the water of life." Drink ye *deep* of same, that the healing you each may administer to others may flow as His love through thee! For love healeth the wounded; it binds up the brokenhearted; it makes for understandings where differences have arisen. For *God is* love.

[Background: Hebrew, singer. She and her husband-to-be became strong supporters of the Cayce work and had many personal readings. She also had a very challenging relationship with her future mother-in-law.]

Reading 938–1

(Q) *Am I justified in my dislike for the woman who upsets me so much?*

(A) Justified by what? "As ye do it unto those, my children, ye do it unto me."

There should be more love, more loving indifference shown by self, in respect to the individual. For ye have much to meet together. Let *Him*—let *Him* direct thy justifying. "I will repay saith the Lord."

Then, art thou justified? Stand rather justified before Him, in thy dealings, in thy judgements, in thy activities.

For to think, to act, as if *thou* art lord or master is to belittle and degrade thine better self.

(Q) *Has she any real reason for talking and acting the way she does?*

(A) These arise from experiences where associations have made for the abilities of the self being such that the lauding by others has brought torments to the other. Hence be patient; be loving *with* those that would do thee harm. It is but pouring coals of fire upon their heads, and will bring to thee the greater satisfaction.

For if *thou* dost conduct *thyself*, thy thoughts, thy acts, so that the Lord be on *thy* side, who can be against thee?

Act the more often, then, that though they make for discourteous, unkind remarks, the Lord loveth rather him that can speak *gently* to those that would do thee harm.

(Q) *Will she aid or interfere with my future happiness?*

(A) Dependent upon the manner in which the self *meets* those experiences. Turn—*turn* the other cheek, when thy enemy, thy friend, would smite thee. Let the Lord have His way, and ye will find it will turn to a *helpfulness* in the experience.

[Background: Project auditor, Protestant. This was a check life reading on an Egyptian incarnation and its influences on her present associations. Part of her counsel included how she could overcome tendencies in her relationships that had originated in her prior incarnations.]

Reading 2390–7

Thus the lesson to the entity: Do not let regret, jealousy, become a part of thy mental experience. These ye can control in thy mental self.

Not always easy, but putting that purpose forth as indicated—the hope, the desire, the faith in the promise of Him—He may take away thy burdens . . . the Master, who is the way, mind and body, spirit and soul, may become one with that purpose of Creative Forces; that may not disintegrate with activity, but grow—as love—in demonstration; and feeds not upon the weaknesses or the miseries of others.

Keep that faith.

Ready for questions.

(Q) *In what way do the regenerations of that period tie in with my present life, and how can I best use them constructively?*

(A) As indicated. Trust not in those things that are of the material making, but in those that are ever creative; letting those activities of self-indulgence or self-gratification not ever become the rule, but rather purposefully building towards the consciousness of the Christ-presence.

(Q) *In previous readings it has been given that I can recall certain experiences from past incarnations. In order that I may become more conscious of these experiences and they will help me to develop spiritually, please give instructions as to the method of meditation that will be best for me.*

(A) As indicated in that given, when ye would meditate—or when ye would sleep, put all hate, all jealousy, all regret, from thy mind—by filling the mind with the consciousness of the Christ-power. For, as He hath given, each soul is in that consciousness it has builded—by what it has done *about* universal consciousness in its experiences.

Thus, as the entity knows itself, its weaknesses, its faults, put them away; trusting in Him. For His promises are to bring to the remembrance of all, that which will enable them to *ever* glorify God in their dealings with others.

Thus, as given, to him who hath much, much may be given. To him who hath much, of him much is required.

As others will, and do consciously and unconsciously look to thee—for a look, for a word, for an expression—so live as to ever be to others one that walks and talks oft with Him. This will enable the entity to fulfill that purpose for which it came into this experience.

[Background: Stockbroker, Protestant. He was seeking advice as to how to help his ward (631) and whether or not finances he was eventu-

**ally anticipating from an inheritance could be used for the same pur-
pose.]**

Reading 1793-1

EC: Yes, we have the body, the enquiring mind, [1793]; and those
conditions, those desires and purposes relative to [631].

In giving advice and counsel regarding such associations and relations, desires and purposes and wishes, many phases of man's experience and man's endeavors should be taken into consideration—rather
than saying alone "I will."

Rather are the circumstances in the present much in that manner as
has been said, "Man's extremity becomes God's opportunity."

And unless one can truly say within, "Thy will, O God, be done in
me, through me," and then the life, the activities, the associations with
the fellow man day by day in accordance with that prayer, that supplication—there is little hope for such an entity or body . . .

Then let thy activity, thy prayer, thy supplication be in *those* directions, that:

"As Thou seest, O God, use Thou me; that there may come to thy
children who seek to know in this material experience the greater truth,
the greater mercy Thou may show; not to be used in self-indulgence, in
self-honor or glory, but rather in self-effacement; that the glory Thou
hast shown in Him may be manifested in the lives and hearts, and in
the bodies of these Thy children!"

This is the manner, then—through prayer, though meditation; not as
one shutting himself away from its fellow man, but knowing that it is as
ye do it unto the least of thy neighbors, thy brethren, thy fellow men
day by day, that ye bespeak of the fountains of purposes within thine
own heart and soul respecting thy Creator!

Then, not by might and by power but by the love that thou hast for
thy fellow man, may this thing be accomplished in thy desire, in thy
endeavor; that these be made one with God's purposes with thee *and*
thy ward!

**[Background: Retired professor, Protestant. This was a life reading in
which the individual counsel included information on how to become**

more consciously aware of his relationship to God.]

Reading 2246-1

The records each entity makes are written or impressed upon time and space; and through patience one may attain to the awareness or consciousness of same in one's own experience.

Thus may the relationships of the entity and the universal consciousness, or God, become more and more a conscious reality. Not that it may be even describable in words. For, words are merely a means of communicating ideas to one individual from another, while universal consciousness with Creative Forces is rather the awareness that bespeaks of life itself. And life in every form is the manifestation of that force called God.

Yet, as was given in those admonitions by Him—who in the flesh was a manifestation, or became the manifestation of that God-consciousness in the material world—"In patience ye may become aware of, or awakened to, thy soul. In patience, and living in that consciousness, I may bring to your remembrance all things from the foundations of the world."

These are indications, then, that this entity in itself may—if it chooses—come to that awareness of its relationships to that universal consciousness, that Christ-likeness which is manifested by the relationships or dealings one with another.

For as each soul—not the body but the soul—is the image of the Maker, so with the awareness of the soul-consciousness there may come the awakening to the realization of the soul's relationship with that universal consciousness, as is promised in Him.

Thus the records of each entity are a part of the universal consciousness, and "Inasmuch as ye did it unto the least of my little ones, ye did it unto me." These are the channels, these are the records then that ever stand as that angel before the throne, that there may be intercession. For, as the spirit of the Christ is one, and the individual entity in its manifestations of thought, purpose and desire makes its awareness one with that consciousness, so may that soul awareness come. For, ye find thyself body, mind, soul. These three bear witness in the earth. And the Christ Consciousness, the Holy Spirit *and* thy guardian angel bear witness in the spirit . . .

Thus is each soul, each entity, a co-creator with that universal consciousness ye call God.

[Background: School counselor, Catholic. This was a life reading in which the individual was especially interested in her present-day relationships with various individuals and family members.]

Reading 2629-1

These we choose with the desire and purpose that this may be a helpful experience for the entity; not only to encourage the entity in the present experience but that it may better fulfill the purpose for which it entered this sojourn; that it, the entity, may better be a channel of blessings to others—which has been and is the entity's intent and purpose.

For, as there is builded in the innate and manifested experience of each entity, these become at variance oft to that ordinarily comprehended. For, the awareness or consciousness in the material plane has been and is given an individual soul as an opportunity for growth; which has been indicated by Him who is the way, the truth, the light— that was shown in the experience of the entity in those closer relationships with that activity in this material plane.

Those consciousnesses or awarenesses between the manifestations materially, by law only—and that as has been manifested by an individual entity, are put into practice in that interim. Thus does the individual entity grow. Thus does it manifest. Thus the reason, the purpose for varied experiences in materiality as is known in the present consciousness.

He hath not willed that any soul should perish, but hath with every trial, every temptation, prepared a way, a means of escape—or for correction; which was and is manifested in Him . . .

For, as indicated, the ability for the application of love as related to tolerance is the greater virtue in the entity's present experience.

Thus in thy dealings with others, magnify their virtues, minimize their faults. For, even as thy Lord condemned no one, even as He forgave, so would you forgive. Even as thou counseled with those in that period, acting as the teacher, the instructor, in the abilities for practical application of life and to meet same in others . . .

And know today there is no other than that found in the admonition given by Jesus of Nazareth, Jesus the Christ—"If ye believe in God, believe also in me." Hence He is that to which the mind of the individual entity responds. He is the way, the Mind is the way. And as the mind dwells upon the fruit of the spirit—faith, hope, gentleness, kindness, patience—it may blossom into that which brings the hope of man, the confidence in his brethren, the faith in his God . . .

(Q) What has been my relationship in past incarnations with [2174]?

(A) Acquainted in the Palestine experience, as from afar. Here, the entity [2174] knew of and blessed the entity for its life and purpose. In the Egyptian, closely related. For, there were . . . the collaboration of the efforts in the teaching principles, as would be called in the present; that is, the selection, the counsel with individuals as to special service or activities, through that particular period of man's unfoldment.

(Q) Please give that which will help to elucidate that relationship for our future working together?

(A) As the purposes have been, good. As the advice and counsel of each have been, good; though they differ in some manners of application. Let each study to be one in purpose, even as He is one; they each in their own sphere making their contribution in a united effort to the glory of Him who is the Giver of all good and perfect gifts. Not as an abstract experience, but as a living experience. For, know, the Father God is God of the living, not of the dead.

Let the dead past bury its dead. Let the living past bloom into that activity in which it may bear fruit in Him.

Let thy light so shine in each life ye meet, that they—as they do—take thought that thou hast oft walked and talked with Him, who has promised, "If ye love me, ye will keep my commandments, and I and the Father will come and abide with thee."

These are not idle words in the experience of any soul that seeks His face. For He hath promised ever, "Though ye be afar, if ye call I will hear—and answer speedily. If ye will be my children, I will be your God."

This is not of old, but a living thing in the hearts and souls of those today. For the fact of thy consciousness in a material world. Though troubled and a blood-stained world, thy prayer, thy blessing may bring a new hope, and may blossom into joy on earth, peace among men.

We are through for the present.

[Background: Retired laboratory researcher, widower. This was a mental and spiritual reading in which he sought to clarify those things in his life that were hard to understand from a rational point of view.]

Reading 2879-1

Man finds himself a body, a mind, a soul. The body is self-evident. The mind also is at times understood. The soul or the spiritual portion is hoped for, and one may only discern same from a spiritual consciousness.

The body, the mind and the soul are as the Father, the Son and the Holy Spirit—just as infinity in its expression to the finite mind is expressed in time, space and patience. These are exercised in the consciousness, and yet only the spiritually discerning may interpret. *Spiritually* there becomes no time or space, for they—like the Father—are one. But in man's application they become as one, in the Father, the Son and the Holy Spirit.

Thus in man's interpretation of God's revelation to man through the written word, there becomes confusion at times, and it does not always seem to fit or coordinate from a rational point of reasoning.

Yet man discerns, as within himself, that his body has its attributes, its functionings, its phases of expression. It grows in physical, in the mental, and in its ability of spiritual discernment, through the application of the truths, the tenets, the laws of the spirit, of the mind, and of the body.

There may be, then, definite interpretation. These are not all the laws, to be sure. For, as the body, there are many organs, many functionings. Yet if there is a coordination of these, there is the physical, mental and spiritual discernment of that the body–entity experiences.

In the discerning, then, of the laws—these become one in Him. The first is then as He gave—"Thou shalt love the Lord thy God with all thy body, thy mind, thy soul; thy neighbor as thyself." This, then, is all-inclusive, yet may be better discerned in the study and the application of the tenets set in the thirtieth (30th) of Deuteronomy by the lawgiver in his admonition, in his summing up of the laws, the ordinances that had been indicated for a peculiar people, set aside for a purpose—as a channel through which there might be the discerning of the spirit made manifest in flesh.

Hence it is reminding man that today, now, every day, there is set before him good and evil, life and death. Man does not find other than that answer outside himself as expressed in that spiritual discernment, "My spirit beareth witness with thy spirit."

Thus, as the lawgiver interpreted, "Lo, He is within thee." Man's discerning of that he would worship, then, is within self; how that he, the individual entity, makes manifest in his dealings daily with his fellow men that God is, and that the individual entity is—in body, in mind, in soul—a witness of such; and thus he loveth, he treateth his brother as himself.

Such an admonition has in man's interpretation oft put God, the mighty, the Lord, as far away. And yet he recognizes, if he accepts this admonition of the lawgiver, that He is within self.

This is more clearly demonstrated and interpreted in the words of the Master himself—"In my Father's house are many mansions"—many consciousnesses, many stages of enfoldment, of unfoldment, of blessings, of sources. And yet God has not willed that any soul should perish, but has with every temptation, every trial, prepared a way of escape—or a way to meet same; which is indicated here by the Creator, the Maker of heaven and earth and all that in them be.

Thus as He declares, "Behold I stand continuously before the door of thy consciousness, of thine own mansion. For thy body is indeed the temple of the living God." And there He has promised to meet thee. There ye make ready. There ye entertain. There ye meditate upon those influences, those choices ye make day by day.

He, that Christ Consciousness, is that first spoken of in the beginning when God said, "Let there be light, and there was light." And that is the light manifested in the Christ. First it became physically conscious in Adam. And as in Adam we all die, so in the last Adam—Jesus, becoming the Christ—we are all made alive. Not unto that as of one, then. For we each meet our own selves, even as He; though this did not become possible, practical in a world experience, until He, Jesus, became the

Christ and made the way.

Thus He became the first of those that within self arose to righteousness. Thus may we, as individuals—as we apply ourselves—become aware of that abiding presence as He promised—yea, as He maintained—"If I go away I will send the spirit of truth, the spirit of righteousness, and he shall *abide* with you. And I and the Father will come."

Seek ye then to walk with Him. That peace He giveth thee. Not as the world knoweth peace, but as His peace that openeth the door of understanding, of comprehension, of how God maketh peace with man through the law of love. For He *is* law. He is love. He taketh away not the law, but manifesteth love in that He fulfilled the law, in that He gave Himself for that edict, "In the day ye eat thereof, ye shall surely die."

Yet in the day that ye accept Him as thy sacrifice and *live* thyself according to His precepts, *ye* become reconciled—through Him—to the Father, and He—too—walketh and talketh with thee.

Study, then, to show thyself approved unto that as thy ideal.

As to the choices ye make—remember, as He gave, "Who made me a judge of my brother? Who is my brother? He that doeth the will of the Father."

What is the will? "Love one another, even as I have loved you."

2

●

Overcoming Life's Challenges, with Jesus as the Pattern

[Background: Writer, Protestant background, spiritualist. This was a physical, mental, and spiritual reading in regard to challenges she was experiencing. She had complained of bitterness and struggles and terrible lessons she had experienced in her associations with others.]

Reading 954-5

Confusion is often caused, then, and is ever caused unless there is an ideal drawn or accepted by which all of these conditions, all of these experiences—whether physical, mental or spiritual—may be judged; or from which conclusions may be drawn.

Otherwise we are measuring ourselves *by* ourselves, and this becomes unwise. For it again leaves confusions as to what is another's standard.

But know that as ye are body, mind and soul, some portion of this trinity evidently is a part of a universal consciousness; or is accustomed to being, or may be acquainted with being on speaking terms even with that which is a universal consciousness.

There then cannot be one measure for you and another for I, but rather is it of such a nature that it takes hold upon all that is, all that was, all that may ever be. For that consciousness is a part of same.

Who, then, is the author of that awareness, of that consciousness? That which is without thyself? or that which is a part of thyself, that is also a part of that universal consciousness?

Hence as has been given by Him, we may be—an individual entity may be—aware of and yet not a part of that harmony that *is* the birthright of all who oft commune with that universality of good—and right—and harmony!

Then whatever may be the form that partakes of those measures as to guide or direct one in these choices, ye know that it becomes and is thy deeper concept of that universal, that continuous hold upon consciousness itself.

Know that it may partake of or take on that image of the imp. For who hath not in some experience or some consciousness seen himself as such, with all the attributes of what the name itself implies!

And again, who hath not felt the pangs of disappointment, of discouragement, of that anxiety in which it seemeth so useless!

It is because the self has become enmeshed or entangled in the desires of the body, without full consideration of the mind and spirit that knows no *end!* and thus confuses the spiritual, the mental, the physical self.

Then the judgement, then the ideal, is that of the universal love, universal consciousness—that as was and is, and ever will be, manifest in Him, even the Christ—as was shown in the flesh in the *man* called Jesus!

Then when doubts and fears arise, when discouragements and disappointments come—yea, when joy of body or mind or soul is thine—ask thyself the question: "What would Jesus do?"

For if ye do that (and ye will, if you will choose), ye may have—ye *do* have His promise. And remember that there is nothing in heaven or hell, in body, in mind or in spirit that He hath not experienced. And He hath given, "I am thine—I stand at the door and knock." Saith He, "Whosoever will, open thy heart within—I will abide, I will come in and abide; and as I and the Father are one, so may ye and I be one—that the *father* may be glorified in thee, in the *manner* in which ye deal with thy fellow man."

Then, put Him not to shame by speaking, thinking or acting unkindly to thy fellow man. For "Inasmuch as ye do it unto the least of these, my brethren, ye do it unto me," saith He.

It is from that premise, then, my child, that we would give thee thy answer to thy problems, now!

Then take each of them to Him and talk with Jesus about same!

Ready for questions.

(Q) *Please analyze my life path as it now appears and tell me where its most constructive work lies now. What progress is being made toward the order "Make thy paths straight"?*

(A) This ye may better do than any source or channel that would analyze same for thee. For that which troubleth thee today, tomorrow may be as chaff in the wind—yea, may be as burning flax.

Rather as has been given of old: *Use that thou hast in hand today,* and tomorrow that as is necessary will be given thee.

For He will not fail thee! As He hath said, "Though the heavens and the earth may pass away, my word shall *not* pass away!"

Then as the kingdom is within, it is there—in the temple of thine own body, which is the temple of the living God—in which ye, thyself, *must* worship, must meet thyself and the problems of the moment. Then it is there, with Him whom ye would serve!

Whom then, this day, will ye serve? The Lord thy God, or thyself, or fame, or fortune, or any of the attributes of the material world? Knowest thou not that He knoweth what ye have need of before ye ask? But in the asking does the blessing come to thee, and in the asking and in the doing is the glory of the Lord shown to thee! . . .

(Q) *Please give some thought or meditation as help to overcome results of the recent terrible crisis.*

(A) Just as has been given:

O God! Not my will, not my purpose but thine!

Remember the prayer as He gave.

If possible let this cup pass from me, but not my will—thine O God be done in and through me! Here am I, Lord—use me! Though it break my body, though it purge my soul, use me and let me not abuse Thy promises but make them mine—day by day!

[Background: Writer, radio broadcaster, Protestant. This was a life reading in which Cayce counseled her on how to deal with present-day turmoil.]

Reading 1472-1

EC: Yes, we have the records here of that entity now known as or called [1472].

In giving the interpretations of these, we find these are those that may be helpful in the experience of the entity through the present sojourn.

These are beautiful in many of the experiences, yet the more turmoil may appear to be present in this present sojourn.

For the entity has come a long way, and oft grows weary with the burdens not only that become a part of self's experience but that apparently are unburdened and yet burdened upon the entity, in its dealings with those about self.

Remember, though, that these *are* but that which is a part of the experience; for those whom He loveth, those He holdeth dear in their dealings with the fellow man.

For He hath indeed given His angels charge concerning thee, and He will bear thee up—if ye will faint not but hold to that purpose whereunto thou hast purposed in thy tabernacle in the present.

For know that His temple in thee is *holy*; and thy body-mind is indeed the temple of the living God . . .

Yet know in the awareness that ye will find more and more that the *truth* indeed sets one *free. Not* to convention, of the material policies or activities, but in *spirit and in truth!*

For God looks upon the purposes, the ideals of the heart, and not upon that which men call convention . . .

And in the present those abilities arise from its desire, from its hopes to put into the word of the *day*, the experience of the day, in all phases of human experience, *lessons*—yea, symbols, yea tenets—that will drive as it were *home*, in those periods when the soul takes thought and counsel with itself, as to whence the experiences of the day are leading—as to whether they are leading to those activities that are the fruits of the spirit of truth and life, or to those that make for selfishness, and the aggrandizement of material appetites without thought of those things that are creative and only make the pure growths within the experience of others.

Hence whether it be in jest, in stories, in song or poem, or whether in skits that may show the home life, the lover—yea, the weary traveler yea the high-minded, and they that think better of themselves then they ought to think—*these* abilities are there. Use them. For He, even as then, will bless thee with His presence in same. And what greater assurance can there be in the experience of any soul than to know that He—yea, the Son of Mary—yea, the Son of the Father, the Maker of heaven and earth, the Giver of all good gifts—will be thy right hand, yea thy heart, thy mind, thy eye, thy heart itself—if ye will hold fast to Him! . . .

(Q) Why do I get so little love, consideration and appreciation from those to whom I pour out the most service and devotion?

(A) Study that which has been given thee relative to such, and ye will see that it is patience ye must learn, that ye must add to those virtues that have made thee ever the burden bearer for the many throughout those periods when the awakenings were coming.

Faint not because of thy loneliness, for who can be alone with His love, His promises abiding with thee!

These may make for a blooming into activity in thy experience, and *will*, if ye will give expression more and more to those promises that are thy very own.

For He, as He hath promised, may bring to thy remembrance *all* things—from the foundations of the earth. Know the Lord is nigh; and that those who keep watch, who keep faith *with* thee, are even as those of old—when there are the hundreds, yea the thousands that have never bended the knee to Baal, but as thee—only need that light, that assurance that He *is* the guiding light!

(Q) How can I help my daughter, the entity now known as [. . .]?

(A) Be not overanxious. Ever be ready rather to give an answer for the faith that lieth within. Not as argumentive, but as that which has been, which is, which ever will be the assurance to thee of the faith, the love that conquers all . . .

Let thy deeper meditation be, in thine own way, but as these thoughts:

Lord, my Lord, my God! Thy handmaid seeks light and understanding! Open to my mind, my heart, my purpose, that which I may use in my daily service, my daily contacts, that will be more and more expressive of Thy love to the children of men.

[Background: Executive, IBM, Protestant. This was a life reading in which Cayce counseled him regarding challenges he was having in his professional life. He would later change occupations.]

Reading 1497–1

In giving the interpretations of the records as we find here, we choose that as we find that may be applied in the present experience and becomes helpful in the attaining of that which is soul and mental growth of the entity.

While this will cause a great deal of questioning within self, this is given that the entity—then—may look the more closely within self and indeed experience what has been promised to the children of men who seek to carry right and judgement and God into their daily lives.

Thus the entity may become conscious within of the closer walk with the divine, and thus make such closeness of contact with the universal consciousness as to *experience* much of that which may be helpful from the inferences and inclinations that may be interpreted here from the experience of the entity . . .

Do not judge, though, other than ye would be judged. While these temperaments and tendencies become acute, oft stand aside and—in prayer and in meditation, in thy choosing of activities that would meet the needs of the material circumstances—watch thy own self pass by.

Look within, as given, and *see* what have been the promptings that have induced thy activity.

And know that God *is*, and is the Maker, the Ruler of the universe; and He is not mocked, for whatsoever a man soweth, that he must also reap.

And though thy companions, though thy associates, though thy contemporary associates in thine own fields of endeavor or expressions, resort to unfair practices or measures to gain a point or an end, know that these must eventually meet *themselves*—even as thine *own* activities must be met.

For it *is* the law of love, of hope, of patience, of longsuffering, of kindness, of gentleness, that *will* succeed, that *will* bring its fruit in due season.

For He is mindful of the sparrow. How much more, then, is He mindful of His children, His companions that He would have as a portion of His very *self . . .*

(Q) *I now feel frustrated and hindered by dishonesty and injustice which I am not disposed to fight with its own weapons—nor cope with, as I would now desire to, due to present economic uncertainties. May I have specific advice as to a course of action in dealing with my present difficulties?*

(A) As has been indicated, in the manner in which there are thy dealings with thy fellow man ye are thus dealing with thy concept of thy God.

These as to definite applications, as has been given, must be sought within; in meeting these steps day by day. For as ye apply thyself today, in the knowledge thou hast, to the best of thy ability, to the fulfilling of thy purposes to be a channel to make known the love of God, then as ye apply same the next step is shown thee—as ye seek from within.

(Q) *Will you now indicate to me definite lines of action or procedure, with regard to my present situation, to effect the realization of my hopes for achievement?*

(A) Carry on in the ways that have been set before thee, making those preparations for the abilities to be the greater service in those fields of activity that have been indicated may become a part of thy material experience during this present sojourn.

(Q) *What do I lack, both in my inner consciousness, in my habits of thinking and attitude to deal with my problems successfully?*

(A) As has been indicated, take the more often the God–Consciousness into thine own deeper meditations. For He will walk and talk with thee.

These are not, then, faults nor fault–finding. More surety in self, the more study of that which has been or may be drawn by inference, by example, and then by practical application ye may meet thy problems within thine own experience.

[Background: Teacher, Protestant. This was a mental and spiritual reading that was requested to be a source of help to herself and others "in these difficult times."]

Reading 2174-3

Considering the problems of the times, and those that are a portion of the entity's experience—each entity—as this entity—has a part to play, as it were, in meeting those varied problems that are arising; not only in the minds and experiences of those who are as companions, associates, friends, but—with this entity—in the lives and activities of many who are to be the leaders, the instructors, the guiding lights for the future generations. For, it is such groups who adhere to those tenets, those principles as have been indicated in that given, that are to lead peoples—everywhere—to the knowledge of the closeness, the oneness as may be attained in so doing.

There are those activities that will bring such awarenesses, by the own force and power of might as set in motion by all the characters of influences that go to make up those problems and activities of the entity.

Yet with that singleness of purpose which has prompted those activities in the past, there will open many a door for the sustaining help—in the mental as well as in the material ways.

Such help, as we find, comes by the very sincerity of purpose; which, as has been indicated, is given and *is* activative in the life of this entity . . .

(Q) *Please explain the difference between laying all on Him, and through inaction shirking one's task, and seeking thru action to find His way.*

(A) It is like that just indicated—as to how one analyses self in regard to any given problem or condition.

What is the purpose in the individual or self's relationship! Is it that there may be gratified an idea in self, or to be *without* self to the glory of *good* as in Him?

Or, to put in another manner: To lay all on Him is to be willing to say in self, "Not my will but Thine be done. Use me as *thou* seest fit." While, working out to His glory in self is, "Lord, I am willing—but let me tell you how!"

(Q) *Is my inactivity due to lack of confidence in myself, enhanced by the palpable insecurity of the group? How may I get a clearer perception of His will?*

(A) Enter into the better communion with Him, *in* the within-self. This will give the better understanding, the better awakening.

(Q) *I have used service as love's symbol, but somewhere have missed. Where?*

(A) *Who* is to find fault? He did not! He does not! He only gives, ever—

"Listen—listen to that within—I will speak and direct the way."

Reserve nothing within—as to purpose, as to individuality or as to personality; but wholly for love, for service. For, "He that will be the greatest among you will be the servant of all."

(Q) How may I know when the will to a course of action is justifiable, or when I am forcing my own personal will which may lead to inaction which is equally unjustifiable?

(A) By the listening within—there is the answer. For, the answer to every problem, the answer to know His way, is ever within—the answering within to that real desire, that real purpose which motivates activity in the individual.

These appear at times to become contradictory, of course; but know—as the illustration has been used here—attunement, atonement and at-onement are *one*; just as the inner self is that portion of the infinite, while the self-will or personality is ever at war with the infinite within—for the lack of what may be called stamina, faith, patience or what not. Yet each entity, each soul, knows within when it is in an at-onement.

[Background: Businesswoman, Protestant, interested in Christian Science. This was a life reading. She was experiencing challenges in her marriage.]

Reading 2427-1

In giving the interpretations of the records as we find them here, these are chosen with the desire and purpose that this be a helpful experience for the entity; enabling it to understand much of that which has been the experience—not only in this present sojourn but through the activities in the material plane.

Thus, knowing self to be itself, in relationships to Creative Forces, the entity may apply self in such a way as to meet, or fulfil, that purpose for which it entered this experience—as one of those privileged through the grace of Creative Forces to manifest in this present experience.

In giving the urges that are latent and manifested, many have been the changes in the experience of the entity in this present sojourn. Oft the entity has asked self, "Why have I been called to meet such an experience as this?"

These are the natural *earthly* approaches to material, mental and spiritual relationships. For—know that the body, the mind, the soul of self are one—even as the Father, the Son, the Holy Spirit are one.

Each phase of self, then, must find in the Creative Forces a reflection of that which it may choose for its directing light at *every* stage of the experiences in material plane.

For, know, He hath not willed that any soul should perish, but hath with every temptation, every trial, given a way, a means of understanding. For as He hath given, "Take my yoke upon you and *learn* of me."

Hence we find, as the Son represents the mind of self, it is then necessary that each soul choose the being of one mind with Him—who thought it not robbery to make Himself equal with God, and who hath called to *every* one, "Be ye perfect, even as my Father in heaven is perfect."

What (ye ask) has this to do with the trials, the temptations, the disappointments that have come into the experience of every individual at one period or another?

Learn, even as it was said of Him; that though He were the Son, even *He* learned obedience through the things which *He* suffered . . .

Disappointments, then in these relationships, have at times brought sorrow, deep thought to the entity.

Again the entity has only found peace when returning to that which has been indicated, "Though He slay me, yet will I love Him the more." Or, as given again, "Unto *whom* shall I go? Thou, O Lord, hath the words of eternal life."

These as we find are the various phases of urges latent from the astrological aspects, that bring the deeper urges—as indicated from the high mental ability, the *strength* of the entity in its reliance *wholly* upon the truth, the promise, the love that is indicated in Him.

Hold *fast* to that which has so oft been determined in thyself, and ye shall find peace, harmony—as is His promise—coming unto thee!

There *cannot* be happiness or joy save when self has found peace *within* self.

Condemn not, that ye be not condemned; but as that peace He hath promised comes to thy consciousness, more and more the material environs will become in keeping with the *needs* of that to *make* thee *aware* of His presence abiding with thee.

**[Background: Housewife, Protestant. This was a life reading and in-
cluded a question regarding creating harmony in her marriage. She and
her first husband were divorced within five years, and she later married
again. She and her second husband had many problems, which they
eventually worked out.]**

Reading 263-4

(Q) What can I do to help the financial condition of my family?

(A) Remove any thought or purpose or cause of anxiety for self from
the others, and there will be made the harmonious experiences that
will aid self and others in *making* for the necessary *material* activities in
the experience.

(Q) Am I psychic? If so, how may I develop so that I can be of the greater use?

(A) Every soul is psychic, and the entity is above the ordinary from
the experience. The abilities have been used erringly. Turn them to the
light. Let the light of the truth guide thee, as in His promises that "I will
abide with thee and bring to thy remembrance *all things* from the beginning." Then meditate upon that the Lord thy God, thy Christ, would
have thee do. Let thy prayer day by day be:

*Here am I, Lord! Purge Thou me from all unrighteousness. Make me a greater
channel of blessings to everyone day by day; not my will but Thine, O Lord, be done
in and through me.*

**[Background: Widow, writer, Protestant. This was a physical and mental
reading in which she sought answers to questions regarding the "physical welfare and the mental decisions" she had to make at the time.]**

Reading 1152-13

When doubts and fears and turmoils arise, then turn to Him; knowing, as He hath promised, He is able to keep that which is promised. For,
only in overcoming the world, death, hell and the grave, was he able of
or capable of, willing to be that direction, that security, that safeness as
He hath promised.

Let the mind, the body, the purposes, the hopes, then, be centered in
Him; who hath given, "If ye love me, keep my commandments, and I
will come and abide with thee always," giving that peace, not as the

world knoweth peace but that safe security, that understanding that brings harmony in the activities, in the relationships, in the meeting of every phase of the experience in this material world.

Know, as He hath indicated in His life, that if there is the determination, the desire to do good, then disturbances as of the world arise. But in thy choice of manner and means of activity, of service, let it be even as He gave, "The prince of this world cometh, but he has no part in me."

So live, so think, so do, that fear, doubt, disturbance of any nature may be wholly cast out; through the trust, the faith, the hope in Him.

[Background: Housewife, Protestant. This was a mental and spiritual reading in which she sought help concerning the anxiety and worry she felt about the welfare and safety of her son, who was a private during World War II.]

Reading 602-7

EC: Yes, we have the body, the enquiring mind, [602].

In giving a mental and spiritual reading, especially in relationship to those confusions and disturbances in the body and mind—many varied phases of the mental and spiritual life, the mental and spiritual experience, must be taken into consideration.

To be sure, there is builded within the consciousness of the entity, [602], an aversion to strife, to war, and to all phases of military activity. The entity should consider, however, if this consciousness bears the same relationships to all other forms of activity that may more subtly destroy the soul, rather than the body.

Remember, there has been given, "Fear rather him who may destroy body and soul than he who may destroy the body alone."

In an hour of trial, when there are influences abroad that would change or mar, or take away that freedom which is the gift of the Creative Forces to man; that man might by his own innate desire be at-one with God, the Father, as was manifested in Jesus, the Christ; there should be the willingness to pattern the life, the emergencies, the exigencies as may arise, much in the way and manner as the Master indicated to each and every soul.

According to the pattern of the life, as He gave, one should ever be able to give the evidence of the hope and faith that lies within the individual.

One should ever be able and willing even to lay down the life for the principles that may live as He indicated; that of freedom not only from the fear of servitude, not only from the dictates as to the manner in which love, sacrifice, obedience may be administered to the faith and hope that lies within him, but that the whole earth may indeed be a better place for an individual, for those that are to come to reside in.

To be sure, taken as a personal application, these become in a manner necessarily as of self. But self, too, may needs be offered on the altar of sacrifice.

When He withheld not His own Son, how can ye ask Him to withhold thine? if it needs be that necessary that the world may know that He, the Father, sent the Son into the earth?

Live in thine own life that which is worthy of acceptance, of that ye ask of the Father; and He will not withhold any good thing from thee.

Are thy principles, thy activities in keeping with His purposes?

This ye may ask day by day:

Lord, show Thou me the way. Let me not in mind, in purpose, in intent, dictate to any: but thou, O God, direct the ways, the purposes.

In that attitude ye may create about thy loved ones, thy friends, thy brethren, that sureness in Him that may bring about the *needs* for that life, that experience of thy son in the vineyard of the Lord.

Know and realize that the earth is the Lord's, with all its turmoils and its strifes, with all its hates and jealousies, with all its political and economic disturbances. And His ways, the Lord's ways, are not past finding out. By living them in the little things day by day may that surety in self, that sureness in Him, be thine. For His promises have been and are sure. And, as His promise has been, "Let not your heart be troubled; ye believe in God," believe also in the Christ, who gave "If ye love me ye will keep my commandments, and I and the Father will come and abide with thee day by day."

So live, then, so think, so act in thy conversation, in thy convocation with thy fellow man, that others may know, too, that the Lord walks with thee.

Then, so instill that hope, that encouragement in the mind and in the heart of thy son that he, too, may live, may look to the Lord for strength, for purpose, for sureness; and that in the peace which is to come there will be the needs for his activity among the children of men, that the way of the Lord may be sure in the earth.

If this attitude is kept—if the Lord be with thee, *who* may be against thee!

Let that mind be in thee, then, as was in Christ Jesus, who boldly claimed His relationship to God, and so lived among His fellow man.

He, too, showed anger at the house of the Lord being turned into a den of those who took advantage of their fellow man. He, too, brought— through that expression, that hope—that knowledge to those that seek His face, that He knows the heartache of disappointment, He knows the heartaches of fear—even as He prayed, "If it be possible, let this cup pass from me—not my will, O God, but Thine be done."

In that attitude, in that pronouncement may there come to thee that strength, that knowledge that ye *can*, ye may trust wholly in the Lord.

Ready for questions.

(Q) *Could he be transferred to some post closer to his home?*

(A) This may be, but is it best? Rather than making the environ by doubts and fears, isn't it better to put it all into the hands and upon the heart of thy Elder Brother? yea, in the hands of thy God? seeking that He use thee and thy body, as manifest in thy son, to bring hope and love and peace to the children of men.

(Q) *Is it best for him where he is?*

(A) As He gave—consider well His answer, the Master—"No man is in this or that position save by the grace of God." Then the opportunities are *where* he is in the present, *using* the knowledge of the material, the mental and spiritual life for the betterment of his fellow man where he is.

That impress, that instill in self.

(Q) *Is there any other branch of the service where he could serve, that would be less dangerous?*

(A) No portion of the service is dangerous if he is put in the hands of God, and the self and the son *live* that as is known! Look upon that condition which disturbs not from the material angle but from the standpoint of a mental and a spiritual blessing to others in the opportunities offered.

(Q) Could he better serve in some defense work outside the military service?

(A) If it had been, would not this have been the place? If what has been given is studied, these questions will be answered. Fill the place better *where ye are*, and the Lord will open the way! Is this not in keeping with His life, His teachings? These are worthy of acceptation. These are worthy of being trusted, of being lived.

[Background: Corporation lawyer, Protestant. This was a business reading in which he asked about his life and work, and about how he could be of assistance to others.]

Reading 877-29

For, these are times and occasions when every effort should be made to preserve the universality of *love* as was and is presented by those who seek the way through *Him*—who is the light of the world!

For He alone has overcome the world—and such must be kept. While there may be many signposts, many roads, many roads that lead to the Cross—the *cross* is that through which *all* gain the greater concept of the purpose of life's expression with human souls endeavoring to seek the light . . .

(Q) I seek direction as to how to clear my debts.

(A) These can be met only by measuring up to that which brings the promise—that is well known in self—from the *sources* of supply—materially, physically.

For the earth is indeed the Lord's, and the fulness thereof. The silver and the gold are his.

When ye measure to that standard where there is needed such for the best mental and soul development, such is—will be—supplied.

(Q) My one and only desire is to do the will of our Father. What is His will for me?

(A) As has been given of old, know that it is not that someone—either from heaven or from over the seas—would bring thee a message, a direction. For it is within thine own self alone that the contact can be made.

Liken it unto the radio, the telephone, the electric light. The current for either is within thine own self. Knowledge of patterns and illustrations of either of these, as material things, may be brought to thy attention. But for self to enjoy that understanding which comes from even the use of these in their material application, self must make the effort, must make the contact, must make the attunement.

For thy body is indeed the temple of the living God. There He has promised to meet thee. There He has promised to make Himself known to thee, His will, His purpose with thee.

That may *not* be supplied by another. If that were true, that it might be supplied by another, why the need of the Son to suffer the death on the Cross, to offer Himself as a sacrifice? He offered it not alone for thyself, for the world, for the souls of men, but for His *own* being!

For, ye—too—are *His* son; and ye, too, are brethren one with another.

Seek and ye shall find, knock and it will be opened unto thee.

We are through for the present.

[Background: High school teacher, Protestant—spiritualistic tendencies. This was a mental and spiritual reading in which the importance of spiritual ideals was stressed as a means of dealing with her life issues.]

Reading 1440-2

For know first, the image must be in the spiritual ideal before it may become a factor in the mental self for material expression.

Hence the purposes for which the entity enters this present experience in the earth, that it may show forth in its dealings with its fellow man the *ideal* manner of meeting not only the material things that have to do with the body–associations but also with the mental and the spiritual. And as has been indicated, and as is known by the body in its experience, it is not what one knows in an abstract manner but what one does about its knowledge, its understanding, in a mental, in a spiritual way and manner, that is to become a portion of the entity's activity, is that which makes for the constructive forces in the experience of this entity, in the experience of every soul.

For a pattern has been given, as the pattern of the Holy One, as the pattern in a more abstract yet material manifestations of same in the wilderness. That the body, self, is then indeed the temple of the living God, that is ideal. For He, the Maker, the Creator, came into a body, flesh and blood, that it might be shown man—yea, might be shown the entity—as to what is the ideal manner to meet every experience.

For as has been given, He was tempted in all points like as we are, yet without error. Yet He bore in the body the sufferings of the body; want, loneliness—forsaken; and all that play upon the emotions of the bodily functions; knowing within self the abilities of self to by the mere word, by the speaking to the influences, eradicate these entirely. Is that thy ideal? If not, why not?

In the spiritual pattern then for self, as for all, what would Jesus do? Under every environ, under every circumstance, what has been His message to thee?

These ye have held fast to, but ye have stood in much the same position as the young ruler that asked, "Master, what good thing—what *good* thing can I do that I may inherit eternal life?" "Thou knowest the law." "These have I kept from my youth." "One thing thou lackest yet—sell all thou hast, give to the poor—and follow me."

Then in thine own self there are the needs to humble thyself before thy fellow man; not as one ashamed. Because the Master was humble before the throng, the mockery, the rulers, the riffraff, and wore the purple robe and the crown of thorns, was He ashamed of His position?

Then humbleness is not being ashamed but rather as He, *knowing* in self that it is that necessary for God's will to be the better, the more perfectly, the more truly manifested in thine own experience!

For He hath not willed that any soul should perish, but hath given even His son as the Pattern—yea, thy brother, Jesus, the Christ—that ye may know what is the way, what is the manner. For *He* is the way, *He* is the vine, and *He* abideth in the Father and ye as the branches abide in Him—as ye *do* His biddings.

If thy friend or thy foe smites thee on the one cheek, do ye revile him because his power and his might is greater than thine? because through the experiences of life the positions are such that he is in the more favorable for some material success? Do ye say, "Lord, Thy Will be done in me, *through* me, that I may be the better channel for the expression of Thy Love in the earth—And as I forgive them, Father, that would do me harm, that would humble me, that would make for the experiences to belittle me—as I forgive them, forgive Thou me of my shortcomings"?

Know that even as the Christ, even as the Jesus—had He withered the hands of those that smote Him because it was in His power, He could *not* be, He would *not* be, thy Christ, thy Savior, thy Lord!

Then as He gave, "Do thou likewise."

These are not in thy experience fables or just trite sayings. That ye sow, that must ye also reap. Because ye have sown good deeds and still find that those who would do thee harm apparently succeed, do ye falter? Yea, how was His experience when the ten stood afar and cried, "Lord have mercy upon us, for we are unclean," and He cried, "Go, show thyself to the priest and ye shall be clean," and in the going they became clean; yet only *one* of the ten returned to say "Thank you, Lord"? Did He bring the leprosy again upon those for their activity, or for their forget-fulness? No; rather did He give, "Love those that despitefully use thee," if ye would know the Lord and His ways with the children of men.

That thy Lord through thy expression of thy faith in the Divine has made thee an instrument of teaching and ministering to others in their search for the way of living, in their search for the manner of expres-sions in the material world in a seeking of knowledge and understand-ing, then temper that ye give with the love of the Father in the ways that the Master gave as to why this or that is done in the relationships with thy fellow man. And then ye will find not only does the way of life become rather as He gave, "Take my yoke upon thee and learn of me, for my yoke is easy and my burden is light," but if ye by the power of thy own might and in thy own knowledge and in thy own wisdom force upon those of thy associations this or that activity, ye have left the power of God out of thyself and thy purposes become as naught!

For might and power are of the Lord. For no man, no entity, no pur-pose in the experience of any soul is existent save by the grace of God that the earth might become His footstool, and the dwelling place of *who*? Those that are righteous within their own selves? No; they that have humbled themselves and are faithful to the trust and purposes that have been put into their ways, into their opportunities for being that channel of blessings to someone day by day.

These shall indeed inherit the earth. For they that love the Lord shall inherit the earth.

That ye love, that ye bow to. For where the treasure is, there the purpose and desires of the heart are also.

Through thine undertakings, through thine experiences ye have been and are endowed with an intuition that becomes what ye term psychic force in thy abilities, in thy powers. If thy soul's abilities are being expended for the gratifying of a material desire, they come to naught. If they are expressed and manifested in such ways and manners as to be to the glory of the Father, to the understanding of thy brethren that they may know the love the Father beareth the children of men, then indeed shall they grow and bring forth sixty, yea an hundred fold—in what? "My peace I leave with you—not as the world giveth peace, but my peace I give unto you"—you that *use*, you that *apply* that power of God in thyself through thy intuition, yea through thy soul force, that thy visions, thy dreams, yea thy powers make thee walk with God! Yet if ye do these for that of lauding or lording thy knowledge, thy abilities over the humblest, yea the greatest, yea the vilest of thy acquaintances, ye do so to thine own confusion, thine own undoing.

For what purpose then entered ye into this experience? That thy earthly father, that thy earthly mother brought by a union a consummation of a material desire the opportunity for thy soul to seek expression again in materiality—for it offered thee the opportunities for thy aid to each of them, their aid, their counsel, their guidance to thee that ye might be the better channel.

For as ye viewed from the ramparts of that inter-between thy activities in the material world, ye found a means of expression of that *thou are—in* the mercy of the Lord!

Then use that thou hast in hand day by day. For that as He hath given thee is sufficient unto the day. And when thou hast used that properly and in the name and in the service of thy Lord, He will give, He will show, He will bear thee up.

For indeed He hath given His angels charge concerning thee, lest thou in thy weakness, lest thou in thy forgetfulness, dishonor thyself, thy Lord, thy purpose, thy desire in entering this experience.

Then, let this be thy watchword:

"*Mercy*, Father-God, *not* sacrifice!" For He hath no joy in sacrifice, He hath no joy in suffering, He hath no joy in disease and sorrow; but ye in thy disturbing influence for the moment forget to thank Him for His mercy, His love, that endureth even when we mock Him.

For His love is divine and overlooketh the shortcomings of those that are weak—or self-satisfied.

Can ye do likewise? Is it asking that ye do other than thy Pattern?

And behold it hath not entered the heart of man to know the beauty, the joy, the peace, the *harmony* that the Lord hath prepared for those that love Him!

[Background: Protestant. This reading offered mental, material, and spiritual advice, especially in regard to a pending divorce and the conditions surrounding the marital relationship.]

Reading 1326-1

For unless there is in the mental self an ideal, just as there was in the consummation of the relationships of the entity, it is merely an idea. But were those activities first impelled by a spiritual insight, that was of a creative force or energy?

Has there been the lack of the thought of self? or rather those experiences in which the ideas respecting the relationships in every form have become rather as forgotten promises, forgotten endeavors even? and the desires for self-domination, self-gratification, self-glorification?

And these have brought and will ever bring, in the experience of each and every entity that allows same to become as the dominant factors in its activities, turmoils and strifes that make the experiences which bring about heartaches and disappointments in the material affairs and relationships of individuals.

But choose thou rather the better way, in knowing that as He hath promised in His relationships of life in the material way, if there is the conforming in self to the ideals that are set by Him, these will bring peace and harmony and understanding in the relationships in every manner.

For if the body-mind holds in the mental activities; in the mental attitudes, the fruits of the spirit, then indeed will the experiences in the physical and material life become easily understood.

And whatever may be the choices of others, let self determine: "Others may do as they may, but as for me—I will serve a living God. I will manifest love, I will manifest patience, I will manifest longsuffering, I will manifest brotherly love."

And in so doing there will come in the daily experience that which will bring from turmoils, strifes, heartaches, disappointments, those promises as He hath given, "My peace I leave with you"—not as the world knoweth peace, but that as satisfies the longings of the soul and makes for that experience in the lives of individuals when the outlook becomes more hopeful in Him, in Life, in thy Brother, in thy associations.

For if ye would have peace, be peaceable. If ye would have friends, show thyself friendly. If ye would be loved, be lovely to those ye know, ye meet, yea to thy enemies, to those that despitefully use you; for in thus doing ye may find that happiness, those promises as thy very own.

And until each soul, each entity, claims His promises as their own and in their daily lives, and their daily associations—manifest them to those they meet—they know not the truth of His promises.

For as He hath so oft given, "Though ye be afar off, if ye will call I will hear—and will answer speedily."

Then, to know those influences, to know those activities, to know the ways of dealing with thy problems day by day:

Affirm—then live it:

I am Thine, O God. Thy promises are unto me. I seek to know Thy will, that I may do and walk in the way Thou would have me go, day by day. Not for myself but that Thou may be glorified in and through the choices that I may make in my dealings with my problems, my fellow man, my conditions in every way.

Then be guided by that which speaks from within, and not by every word of others that would have thee defy this, or demand that, or to feel thou art being mistreated in this or that manner. For if thou art God's, if thou art living in His ways, if thou art doing His biddings day by day, they that mistreat thee, they that condemn thee, they that find fault are finding same with God and not with thee!

The assurance then is within self.

As to how to meet each problem:

Take it to Jesus! He *is* thy answer. He is Life, Light and Immortality. He is Truth, and is thy elder brother.

Not as to who will ascend into heaven to bring thee a message, or who would go over the sea that ye might know of Him, but He is in thine own heart; for He hath given, "Behold I stand at the door and knock."

Will ye open and let Him in? For in *Him* is strength, not in the law, not in the man, not in the multitudes of men, nor of conditions or circumstance. For He ruleth, He maketh them—every one. For hath it not been given or told thee, hath it not been known in thine experience that "He is the Word, He maketh all that was made, and without Him there was nothing made that was made"? And He *liveth* in the hearts and the souls of those who seek to do His biddings.

This, then, is not idealistic—but an *ideal!*

"What would Jesus have me do" regarding every question in thy relationships with thy fellow man, in thy home, in thy problems day by day. This rather should be the question, rather than "What shall I do?"

"Lord, I am Thine, and in Thy ways I would go. Direct Thou me in every way."

[Background: Protestant minister, former civil engineer. This was a mental and spiritual reading in which he sought guidance as to his life and work, after having lost his church.]

Reading 1466-3

Each soul, as is known by the entity, enters an experience for the magnifying of the entity's ideal. For as has been given, He hath not willed that any soul should perish; neither does He seek to bring sorrow, disappointments, heartaches, in the experience of those activities in the earth—save it be for the edifying of the soul.

For whom the Lord loveth He chasteneth, and purgeth *every* one.

These to be sure are known in the experience of the entity, yet how to make these applicable, and to become not reconciled but rather the more active, looking forward to the ability of self to stand in every sense, every phase of the experience, as a channel, a manifestation, a helpmeet for those principles, those ideals that are cherished within the inner self, become then the problems.

These then ye know, these then ye must make practical, make applicable.

Humbleness does not mean, then, degrading nor becoming discouraged when self has been refused that which according to the principle of the self is debased by those that *should* be, are in the position to be, helpful experiences in the affairs of the entity.

But he that finds fault, even when these conditions and experiences come about, is not wise.

Rather know, as *He* has experienced and did experience in the associations with man, even to those periods when they could not watch for one hour.

Ye may not expect, ye may not ask to be above thy Lord, thy Master; but He hath willed, He hath desired that ye be one *with* Him; looking forward to the fruit of that in the spirit that ye sow among thy fellow men.

For love begets love, just as patience and longsuffering beget these in the experiences of those that do same.

And ye know He is not unmindful, and that His promises are sure. These ye have proclaimed, these then ye *must* rely upon.

Not that ye become as idle in the vineyard of the Lord. For He will come and reckon with the keepers of the opportunities that are given to each and every soul.

These then should make rather the entity take courage in the faith, in the promise—and make those promises thy very own!

For He will keep watch with thee . . .

(Q) *How may I keep from becoming discouraged?*

(A) Looking to Him, the author, the finisher of thy faith.

For though He were rich, He became poor that He might know thee and that you might know Him as thy brother, thy Savior, thy Lord—and be one with Him.

For the earth is His, as ye know. Trust in Him and ye will find faith. For the lesson ye are learning is *patience*; and in patience ye become aware of, ye possess thine own soul.

[Background: Catholic. This was a mental and spiritual reading with special reference to life work. She described herself as being sorely in need of help, related to her mind being "absolutely torn to shreds" regarding a decision as to her life's work and whether she should become a nun. She later married a sailor, had a baby, and was very happy.]

Reading 1352–4

. . . each soul enters the earth to meet its own self, in its own shortcomings. Yet there is an advocate with Creative Forces, with God; in
Jesus, the Christ, who has set the example of every nature—and He has
set the example of freedom of speech, freedom of activity; yet bound
within that which is ever constructive. He has not given freedom that is
licentious, or freedom that is self-indulgent, or freedom that does not
consider the needs, the desires, the positions of others; but in the example as is set in Him each soul may find that stimulation for activities
in material associations with others to see not the sordid things of an
experience, not grudges, faultfindings, but rather those that are set as
He hath given—"In patience become ye aware of your souls."

Hence He meets with those who give of themselves for a material
service in that in which they themselves may find the greater heights of
beauty—as in song, in music, and the activities in such. He meets them
in those very influences—as has been given by Him, as to whom He
gave the keys—longsuffering, self-abasement, humbleness, patience.

These be those things in which or against which there is no law, but
they are the fruits of the spirit. Then live them day by day in thy associations with not only thy companions and thy friends, but with thy
foes and with those who even speak despitefully of thee—for they spoke
thus of Him.

Then, if ye will keep those things that have been committed unto
thee, the love of the Father as is shown in the Son, and apply same in
those fields in which thy mind, thy activity may find a more beautiful
expression—in the fields of music, as the pianist or the organist (but
these for service to Him, for the praise, for the glory, for the honor of
Him)—ye will find the greater source of happiness, the greater field of
expression, the greater means of building that in the experience of self
which will bring to *Thee* peace, harmony, freedom in Him, and glory in
thy service to thy fellow men and to thy Maker—through Him!

3

●

Understanding the Ultimate Purpose of Life, with Jesus as the Pattern

[Background: Secretary, publicity writer, Protestant, unemployed, widow. This was a life reading. Her husband, an alcoholic, had recently died, and she was anxious about what to do with her life. Her readings urged over and over again to do whatever she did to the glory of the Lord and not of self.]

Reading 1786-1

For this experience of every soul in the material plane is not mere chance, but the fulfilling of that as was set in motion from the entrance of Spirit into matter; that man may know his true relationship to the Creative Forces.

And that exemplified in the life and experience of the Master is the only manner in which such may be known; for only in the manner in which an individual applies self in his relationships to his fellow man is there materially manifested one's concept or one's glorifying of the Maker.

For, "Inasmuch as ye do it unto the least, ye do it unto thy Maker." . . .

For each has some talent, some activity in which it may excel in its relationships to others above *all others*—for some individuals! Hence know that each soul is as precious in the mind or eyes or heart of God as the other.

Hence we find the marital relationships or love of the opposite sex as something the entity desires to lean upon. And as always has been and ever will be, these prove to be just the opposite; with the tendencies and temperament of a continual finding of fault, and to know that self is right and no one else can be!

These are hindrances. Change them to seeing and knowing that ye must see in those who are thine enemies, in those ye dislike the most, something ye would worship in thy Creator!

For each soul is a portion of that Creative Force, that Spirit of Right and Justice.

And *ye* may be able, *ye* may be the one to cultivate that in the experiences of those who may have apparently harmed thee most!

Have they rather not whetted thee to the realization that there is a work for thy hands?

Truth of itself needs no justification.

Do not continue then to justify thyself or thy stand or thy principles. *Glorify* them rather in that as ye do to thy fellow man!

For what ye are and what ye desire innately for *good* speaks so loud, no one hears what ye say, as to what ye profess in this or that direction.

Thy life is an open book, though ye oft turn some pages down and others ye would blot out.

[Background: Nurse, missionary, nondenominational. This was a life reading. She was an evangelist and traveled around spreading the Gospel. She was told that in one of her past lives she had been an Essene at the time of the birth of Jesus.]

Reading 2608–1

Thus a soul is in the earth, in the material manifestations, as in a school of experience. For, no soul gains knowledge or understanding save through experience.

The experience is not of another's making, but of thine own. For in spiritual truths, His spirit beareth witness with thy spirit—not thy uncle nor thy aunt, nor thy father or mother, but thy soul self.

For, until the Creative Force—or God—becomes a personal experience of the soul it has only been heard of, and the activity more oft is because of what others will say . . .

Good alone lives on. For, good is of God.

All temporal, all physical, all of the three dimensional passes away. Only that which is of spirit, of mind, that is of the holy spirit, of the way, the Son, lives on—for it has then attained in the flesh, in the manifestation.

Thus, as indicated in the beginning, it behooves each soul to so live, to so magnify those influences in the experience that it becomes a growth, the nearer to the more perfect understanding.

In the flesh, or in the experiences, these find reflections in what may be the more often termed the appetites, or the senses of the body, and thus become animate or inanimate, according to the application of such in an entity's experience.

Each soul in its awareness is born into an environ materially, an environ spiritually, an environ that may be of the making or the undoing; dependent upon the will—the birthright, the gift of each soul that it may make itself manifest and one with that Creative Force, and not merely an automaton that would be moved only as it would not.

The ability is given each soul to make its will one with His.

Hence, as the Way ever prayed, ever acted ever lived through the experience, "Not my will but Thine, O God, be done in and through me."

This is the way, this is the understanding to which each soul attains as it journeys through those experiences meeting same.

[Background: This woman and her husband (1215) had "deep convictions" but did not have a religious family. This was a mental and spiritual reading in which she was concerned about her children's spiritual development.]

Reading 1348–1

The *soul* is that which is the image of the Maker, and only in patience—as the Christ gave—may ye indeed become aware *of* thy soul's activity; through its longings, through its convictions, through its experience into the realms of the spiritual undertakings.

How do these come about?

Then how do they apply in thyself?

As ye have been taught, as ye are aware, The Godhead is the Father, the Son, the Holy Spirit. Just as in thyself—as the pattern—the body, the mind, the soul. They are one, just as the Father, the Son, the Holy Spirit are one. They each functioning in coordination or cooperation as one with another become as thy own experiences in a material world, the awareness of the consciousness of that God-force, that Spirit abiding within.

Then, there has been given, there has been shown the way that the Father is mindful of His children; that these as they appear in the earth— yea, thyself—are a portion of His manifestation. Not as an indefinite force, not as an unconcrete thing, not as just a mist, but just as is manifested not only in the Christ but as is manifested in thee—thy desires to do right, thy desires that there be the manifesting of love, of patience, of hope, of longsuffering, of brotherly-kindness, of doing good even when others speak unkindly, when others revile thee, when others say those things that in thy physical consciousness find resentment.

But as He manifests—as a portion of that Godhead that is represented in thee, as *in* thy Mind—then ye become aware that ye are *indeed* a child of the living God, and are in materiality for those purposes of manifesting those very things that are the fruits of the Spirit in thy dealings with thy fellow man.

For as ye measure to thy fellow man it is measured to thee again. This is an *unchangeable* law! For as ye ask for forgiveness, only in those measures in which ye forgive may ye be forgiven. For are ye not seeking to be one with Him? Then only *as* ye forgive may ye *be* forgiven! Only *as* ye show forth love may love be shown forth to thee! Ye cannot rise above that as ye measure, that as ye live. For as the expression of life *is* the manifestation of that love, then in the measure as it metes so is it measured to thee.

Know that as the Mind is represented by the Christ Consciousness, it is the Builder, it is the Way, it is the Truth, it is the Light; that is, through the manner in which the Mind is held.

Not that it denies, not that it rejects, but that it is *made* as one with the purposes He, thy Lord, thy Christ, thy God, thy holy self, would have it be.

Not to the glorifying of the body. For even as He, thy Lord gave, "I can of myself do nothing—it is as the Father worketh in and through me."

Then it is as the body, the mind, the spirit—the motivating forces—coordinant as one with another, *with* the divine law. Ye know the law. What is the law?

"Thou shalt love the Lord thy God with all thy heart, thy mind, thy body; thy neighbor as thyself." This as He gave is the whole law. There is none above that. And ye may, as He has promised, become aware in thy own consciousness of His abiding presence, by the awarenesses that may come to thee as ye meditate, as ye pray from day to day.

Ask and He will give. For as ye walk, as ye talk with Him, ye become aware of His presence abiding with thee.

For this purpose ye came into this experience; that ye might *glorify* that consciousness, that awareness of His presence, of His Spirit abiding with thee.

Ye give manifestations of same in the manner, in the way in which ye measure that love to others about thee day by day.

This do, and ye will know the truth—the truth shall indeed make you free. Not condemning, not finding fault here nor there at any of the experiences; knowing that God is, and that ye must, that ye *will*, that ye *may*—and it is the glorious opportunity, the glorious promise to just be able to be kind, to be gentle, to be patient with thy fellow man day by day!

And the *assurance* comes within thy own self, for His promise is to meet thee in the tabernacle of thy own conscience. For as Jesus said, "Lo, the kingdom of heaven is within *you!*"

Ready for questions.

(Q) *My children's spiritual development leaves much to be desired. How may I help them more?*

(A) With the application of those tenets, those truths day by day ye may bring same within their experiences. It is not longfacedness, it is not "Don't do this," or "Don't do that," but *living* day by day—what? Patience, brotherly love, longsuffering! Be ye rather *joyous* in thy problems, *knowing* that He walks and He talks with you when ye open your heart and mind to His presence.

[Background: This woman was cured of scleroderma, and her case history was included in Thomas Sugrue's *There Is a River*. Although this was a physical reading, in other aspects of her life the woman went through much anguish and depression over an unhappy love affair; later, she moved away and became a music teacher and choir director, married, and led a happy, healthy, and fulfilling life.]

Reading 528-13

Rest sufficiently, play sufficiently, work sufficiently—but *think* constructively!

Take into consideration more often the purposes of the activities; not as the *outward* appearances in thy choir practice but what do such activities stand for? What is the message that is to be given to the world through this channel of singing? The love of the Christ to the world!

Then let it be a personal thing to thee, that He is thy strength, He *is* thy life! For in Him ye live and move and have thy being!

Then let it become a more personal thing; and the more personal His life, His love becomes, the easier, the more beautiful, the more effective the message that will be given in the organ or in the pupil that ye would teach or what—not only to others but to those that convey in song the message of the *living* redeemer, the living Savior!

These being a part, then, of thyself will bring thee *strength*, will bring thee *help*, will bring thee *love*; of which all the other influences are only a part!

Make it then cooperative, and cooperate with that being applied. Let thy life, thy love, thy activities not only be good and well-spoken of but good *for* something; creating that atmosphere, that life, that love, in the experiences of the hearers, that makes more and more the Christ a living thing in thy experience.

[Background: Housewife, Protestant. This was a mental and spiritual reading in which the individual had requested "information, advice and guidance as to her mental and spiritual development and expression."]

Reading 1158-14

For the whole law, as He gave, is to love the Lord thy God with all thy heart, thy mind, thy body; thy neighbor as thyself.

There is not looking then for the message to be descended from heaven by those that may be of this or that thought, but rather as He gave, "The kingdom of heaven is within—Believe thou in me—if not because of my existence because of the works that I do," that ye may do in Him; "for of myself I can do nothing, only as the Father worketh in me."

And in those words as He gave, "In my Father's house are many mansions—if it were not so I would have told you, for I go to prepare a place, that where I am there ye may be also," that ye may *behold* the glory that is prepared for those that love the Lord and His ways with the children of men.

And as He gave, "They that abide in me, the same shall know the Father, for I will come and abide with those that love the Lord and His coming."

These then may become thy experiences. Little may be added.

There has remained within self, it is true, as has been indicated, some questionings. But ye know the way. For as He gave again, "The Lord thy God is not past finding out." It is as ye apply that in thy life in thy relationships with thy fellow man that ye come to know Him as *He is!*

Ready for questions.

(Q) *Is it correct when praying to think of God as impersonal force or energy, everywhere present; or as an intelligent listening mind, which is aware of every individual on earth and who intimately knows everyone's needs and how to meet them?*

(A) Both! For He is also the energies in the finite moving in material manifestation. He is also the Infinite, with the awareness. And thus as ye attune thy own consciousness, thy own awareness, the unfoldment of the presence within beareth witness with the presence without. And as the Son gave, "I and my Father are one," then ye come to know that ye and thy Father are one, as ye abide in Him.

Thus we find the manifestations of life, the manifestations of energy, the manifestations of power that *moves* in material, are the representation, the manifestation of the Infinite God.

Yet as we look into the infinity of space and time we realize there is then that force, that influence also that is aware of the needs, and there is also that will, that choice given to the souls of men that they may be used, that they may be one, that they may apply same in their own feeble, weak ways perhaps; yet that comes to mean, comes to signify, comes to manifest in the lives of those that have lost their way, that very influence ye seek in the knowledge of God.

For until ye become as a savior, as a help to some soul that has lost hope, lost its way, ye do not fully comprehend the God within, the God without.

[Background: Student, a "drop-out," Catholic. This was a physical reading. The individual was gay and went through much torment because of his sexuality. The readings suggested that some of his sexual feelings were actually psychic abilities trying to express themselves and that he should seek guidance from within.]

Reading 1089-7

Hence then the standard or the rule that has been set by the individual as its ideal in its relationships to its Maker and its fellow man becomes the all-important experience of each individual in its dealings with itself and its fellow man.

In Jesus, who became the Christ, you have a pattern, you have an example. Study then to show yourself approved unto that standard. Know that His promises to man, as to his relationships to things in the earth, to things about the individual, to his Maker, to the heavenly Father, are true. For as He gave, "Though the heavens and the earth may pass away, my word shall *not* pass away—but shall be *fulfilled every whit!*"

Then walk circumspectly in the light of thine own understanding. For as you understand and live to that standard, it is acceptable; and as changes come and you are shown the way, you grow in grace, in knowledge, in understanding of what thy Lord hath for thee to do.

You did not come into materiality for an act of a whim, but of your own choice, through the channels open for you. Hence each day, each hour, each association is an *opportunity* for you to know your Maker, your Lord, your God, the better.

Use such opportunities, do not abuse them. Keep the body, the mind, the whole of the intent and purpose circumspect; not as to what others say but as to what your conscience—in prayer, in meditation—may show you. For as He has given, "My Spirit beareth witness with thy spirit." This is the answer then to each soul.

For, "If ye love me, keep my commandments." What is the whole commandment? "That ye love one another, even as I have loved you, even as the Father hath loved thee—ye abiding in me and I in Him."

These be the promises in Him that are safe, sane, peace, harmony, and understanding.

[Background: Writer, Protestant background, spiritualist. This was a follow-up life reading in which she sought additional guidance to enable her to fulfill the purpose for which she entered the earth in this incarnation.]

Reading 954–6

(Q) What general progress am I now making for soul growth?

(A) This might be answered in many ways, and considered from many phases or angles.

The very purposes indicate soul growth; the very desires latent and manifested, in attempting and in being that which is the conviction.

As to soul growth, let this be fully understood:

As indicated to mankind from the beginning, man is a free-willed, a free-purposed individual. Then, as to whether the soul growth is towards the purpose for each entity's experience in the earth must be answered from within self—according to what has been chosen as the ideal, the purposes and aims, and as to *who* and as to *what* is that ideal.

There are many interpretations of soul purpose, or of guiding and directing influences in the material plane, that are extenuations or activities that emerge from the unseen or the inter-between. Here we would give that the ideal should be, for each soul, that proclaimed by Him—who thought it not robbery to make Himself equal with God, and who came into the earth to fulfill that purpose from the beginning; that man through materiality might manifest physical, mental and spiritual influences. Hence through that manifestation as the Galilean, as the Son of man, as the son of Mary, as the Son of God, He fulfilled in the body the whole of the law which had been indicated by those to whom he pointed as being schoolmasters, teachers, interpreters. And He proclaimed that it was not of Himself, but as the spirit of truth might work in and through Him.

So may the individual in the present plane of experience manifest those tenets, those truths that He presented as the way, the manner in which one might attain to soul growth, full awareness, life abundance as expressed and manifested by Him.

That we would give as the ideal.

For this then the entity only has to look within self, to see, to experience that which has been and is the soul growth. Hold fast to those tenets, those principles, if ye would know the way, the truth, the light . . .

(Q) Can you suggest a masterly teacher to help me?

(A) Why seek only a master, or a teacher, when the promise is from Him that "If ye love me and keep my commandments, I and the Father will come and abide with thee"? There may be indicated to and for the entity those influences as may be directed to make, to bring the whole personality oft. But let not such hinder from the keeping of that promise within. Know that thy body is indeed the temple of the living God. There He hath promised to, and there He will meet thee. Hold to that.

[Background: Housewife. This was a life reading. The woman was especially interested in understanding her life's purpose and in receiving guidance as to how she and her husband could have a more positive relationship.]

Reading 2650–1

The first anxiety, the first awareness of which each soul should become cognizant or seek earnestly, is that God is conscious of thee. And the very fact of your own awareness should ever remind thee of this. If each soul would or could become aware of that, how much difference there might be in the choices made day by day!

For, the first awareness would be that *truly* in Him ye live, ye move, ye have thy being; thus the necessity of daily keeping before thee an ideal—spiritual, mental *and* material; realizing that the earth is the Lord's and the fulness thereof.

Peace, harmony, love—Life and all its consequences—are in Him.

What, ye may ask, is the purpose of all this:

He, the Father, being mindful—which should bring to the consciousness the realization that He hath not willed that any soul should perish.

Thus He gives opportunities to those children of His of whom He is mindful.

Then, take heart. Look about self. Be aware of the blessings, the opportunities He hath put in thy way. Use them to His glory, not to thine self-indulgence nor to the gratifying of selfish motives or purposes.

Such is thy purpose in the earth.

From that given it may be indicated that thou hast not always used that in hand to His glory, yet He hath continued to shower His blessings upon thee. Thus in thy application of that thou knowest to do, ever magnify thy virtues in thyself, in others. Minimize the faults that they be put far from thee.

Thou art aware of the physical consciousness that may arise from desire of body, of appetite, of that cultivated in thy daily experience. Thou art aware of the mental abilities of the body, the mind. So are there urges that stimulate these awarenesses in thy conscious experience. Thus all thou art is the result of what thou hast done *about* thy opportunities, thy ideals, here, now; and in those awarenesses in whatever realm of consciousness the soul–entity has been active.

As is experienced in materiality, one may never stand still. For, there is continuous growth, continuous passing of opportunities—for good, for bad. Only good lives on. Bad disintegrates, for it is not of the eternal—but has been and is the application of that which is temporal in materiality. So this, too, will pass away. And as ye grow in grace, in knowledge and in understanding, the truths that may become realities of that being given thee will live *with* thee, constantly.

[Background: This was a group reading for a spiritual group within the Park Place Methodist Church who sought advice as to how they could "best express the spirit of Christ" in their work.]

Reading 5758–1

Thus as the individuals in such a group read, analyze, study and apply those tenets, those truths that were presented by the Christ, they find that the Christ Consciousness must become an individual and yet a living thing within their own individual consciousnesses. As with Him, He found no fault in others. This should be the first premise, then, of each individual; less and less condemning of others and more and more of self manifesting that love shown by the Father through the Son in the material world; that man, through this pattern, through this picture of God, may become a living example, may walk closer in that way of less condemning.

For as each individual realizes, as these tenets may be analyzed, if God had condemned—what opportunity would there be for man to find his way back to God? Thus each individual must do unto others as he would have his Brother, the Christ, his God, the Father, do unto him; and indeed, then, apply first, last and always His "Forgive, O God, as I forgive others. Find fault in me, O God, as I find fault in my brother." Less and less then of self, more and more of perfect love, without dissimulations, keeping that faith. Know that as there is the activity of self, self can only sow the seed of truth. And it will be to each individual as was indicated to the children of Israel. They entered into the Promised Land not because of their righteousness but because of the love of the Father for those who tried, who *tried* to live the righteousness.

Thus each individual may have the try counted as righteousness; not as an excuse, neither as justification. For ye have been justified once for all, through the Christ Consciousness that ye seek.

Then the life, the purpose of the individual, the members of such a Life Group, should be that they may walk closer to the Christ day by day in every way. For His promise has been and is ever to each soul, "If ye will open thy mind, thy heart, I will enter, I will abide with thee." Not as a stranger, but as a brother, as a friend.

In this manner may the group as a group become a power for good, a power magnifying and glorifying the Christ–Life in the church, in the community, in the nation, in the world. For in this showing of the seed of the spirit ye sow, and God alone may give the increase, God alone may prepare the heart.

[Background: This is one of the "Work Readings." It was given at the end of the Fourth Annual A.R.E. Congress to a group interested in bringing spiritual enlightenment to others by presenting the work of Edgar Cayce through the A.R.E.]

Reading 254–87

EC: Yes, we have the group as gathered here, as a group, as individuals; and their interest in how they may be of aid or help to their fellow man.

In giving that as might be helpful to each, in presenting the truths of a spiritual nature as come through the channel here of Edgar Cayce, this might be answered in the one sentence, "As ye have received, so give." If that which has been thine experience has brought thee to a closer understanding of the Divine within, whether from the physical, the mental or the spiritual approach to this work, then of the abundance of thine own experience give out to those that seek; that they, too, may be filled in their own way and manner.

For He has promised, and His promises are sure, "What ye ask in my name, *believing*, ye shall receive."

Many are the channels, as are the minds, of those gathered here. Many make their approach in the manner in which they as individuals have heard, have experienced, have received.

Then all with one purpose, one aim, one desire, yet in their own *way* and manner, should present that they have received. And though someone may laugh or scoff at what ye say, be not dismayed; for so did they at thy Lord.

As to manners or ways as a collective group: What ye *find* to do, with willing hands *do* ye. This may to thine own mind, then, appear to be very indefinite, intangible. Yet is there not set in the experience of each that through some specific office, through some specific group as a part *of* a working unit, there is specific work set for that unit?

As an individual, then, do *thy* part; *realizing* that each and every chain is only as strong as the weakest link. Thou art a portion. Hast thou fulfilled, *wilt* thou fulfill, that as is shown thee by thine own *experience* with same?

What *is* the manner, the way that thou shouldst choose? As He has given, and as ye would ever hear and know, if and when ye love one another even as He hath loved you, then thou wilt be, thou hast been, thou art shown the way. Not that any dictum is set! For He hath made thee to choose; and has said, "When ye call, I will hear—when ye are my children I will be thy God."

So, as the work goes about in its various phases and channels to give help, aid, to this or that phase of its activities, and thou as an individual art called, or thou as an individual art impressed or feel that thou art called, then *act!* Act as thy conscience and thy heart dictate; as thou hast received, so give.

Thus may ye accomplish that which is set before you as a group, as an organization, as an individual.

For unless thy heart, thine mind, is in that ye would do, naught can come to thine efforts. For *this* is the law; as ye sow, so shall ye reap. For man may make *all* efforts, all activity, but only the Spirit of Truth, only God may give the increase, the result. For He *is* the life, He *is* Truth. As ye give expression of same in thine experiences, in those channels, in those promises, in those places of thine *daily* activity, the results only then can and will and do become manifested in the lives and experiences and expressions of those ye contact, as an activative and motivative influence.

For remember ever, the little leavening that ye do day by day leavens the whole lot.

So, let thine mind, thine heart, thine body, be given in *that* manner in which ye have received; so give ye to thy fellow man.

[Background: Chiropractor. This was a mental and spiritual reading in regard to related material affairs and opportunities.]

Reading 683-2

EC: Yes, we have the entity, [683], present in this room, and those experiences and applications of the desires within the experiences through the earth, and those prevalent with their concurrent activities and relation to same in the present experience.

In choosing that, then, in the present, and as to the manner in which the entity may make for the greater soul expression, let the entity turn first to that which has been so oft pointed out; that within the inner self there must be that desire, that expression of desire in such constructive ways and manners as to make for a continued development in a manner of expression that is ever constructive. For from the desire of the heart the mouth speaketh. From the meditations of the soul the hands, the body, the mind, find their manner of manifestation of that which motivates same in material expressions. These are, then the divine laws of activity relating to what has been and is ever given for soul in its expressions, its manifestations, its movements in the earth and its environs. That the man, that the soul in material, finds self continually ever relying upon—and it is seemingly necessary that there be the supply of—material things that make for the expressions of the associations of an entity in its environment is true. Yet such has been met in that given in Him that came into materiality, came into flesh and found the expression among men. Yet, as is spoken of Him, "He came unto his own; his own received him not."

This is as well spoken of this entity as of the man that it is given expression of in that ye read in thine holy places. For each entity, each soul, passes through that realm of experience in the material world that was shown by Him.

Then, ye ask, how, in what manner, in what way is there any benefit to the material individual, the spiritual seeking, the soul's longings in that particular life, that particular experience, that particular manner of death in that man?

That as is promised in Him, "I go to the Father that ye abiding in me (or the manner) may have an advocate with the Father." That ye may as from the beginning approach the throne of grace, the throne of mercy, the access to the first cause. And not through any material soul seeking its way but Him that has from the first abided in the Father. Hence as each soul seeks in this material world through all those conditions, all those environs, all those things that so easily beset the mental mind, the carnal forces, the supply of the material force—as is in exchange for the conditions about each body, each mind for its expression—is supplied in Him. For He is the tree of life; He is the water of life; He is the bread of life; He is that in which each soul may—in its expressions of that He was. He is, he ever will be, in its associations with its fellow man—what He is, was, and ever has been; Peace, Harmony, Glory, Joy, Understanding. For these find their expressions, their attributes in that one does respecting the fellow man. Not sacrifice; for His sacrifice was in faith, that it may be counted to thee as righteousness. Not making for sadness in the sorrow of thine own undoing. For rather has this been expressed that ye in thine inner self may find that peace, that harmony in Him, as ye go about doing; not withdrawing within thine self, as ye go doing; not waiting, not sitting still. For he that doeth the will *is* the will, and becomes one—through Him—in His promises—with The Creative Forces; and a channel, as He is a channel. Others may find that commandment He gave as new ever, to each soul that seeks, "Love ye one another," in such manners that ye prefer even those that would speak evil of thee above thyself, even he that would do thee harm, even he that would speak unkindly, unjustly; ye prefer them and their approach to that throne above thine self. This is the manner. This is the way, His way. For He *is* the way, the truth and the light. In Him is no darkness at all. And if ye would know the light, then hold fast to that thou hast seen and may see in thy kindnesses to thy fellow man; thy gentlenesses, thy brotherly love, thy long-suffering. These make for those fruits that bear in Him the burden of the world. And as ye give expressions of same in thy ministry to thy fellow man, each atom of thyself not only becomes illumined to that strength that ye may impart to the weakened members of a body, but illumining thine own inner self that ye may in so doing also impart to the minds of a such that trust, that faith, that hope in Him; such as to renew that mental force that becomes, with the soul of such, awakened in such measures as to make their portion of the divine in themselves to become like unto the green bay tree, or as the hart upon the mountain as it springs in its youth in spring.

For the heart is gladdened by that light in Him. So may ye find thy ministry in the earth fulfilling that as may be brought to thine own understanding. For He, thy father, thy God, knoweth what ye have need of. And from the abundance of His storehouse doth He supply thy every need. From whence cometh such? As ye measure to thy fellow man, so will it be measured to thee, and *He* putteth it into the hearts of those that ye serve the *abundance* of thy material successes, of thy necessities of the body, of the mind, of the material things in an experience. For thou in so doing putteth thy life, thy portion of Him, into His own keeping. For ye measure same as *He* would measure. And this brings of itself its own reward. For He hath not willed that any soul should see sadness, darkness, nor be troubled *any* at all! But ye in trampling upon

His love, His mercy to those about thee, create (as thou art the portion of Him) those barriers over which ye stumble and fall. But as ye clear the way for thy fellow man so dost *thou* have the clear path that leads to the greater understanding.

In the material associations, in the material connections, then, do with thy might what thy hand finds to do *today*. For sufficient unto the day is the good as well as the evil thereof. For as He hath given in thee that thou may be the channel, the representative, the agent—yea, the very representative in flesh of Him, then act in thine inner self, act in thine outward expression, as though thou wert (for thou art!) His child, and are heir to all the glories *here, now,* of His kingdom. *Not* in the future, not of the past! For in the eternal *now* is He *active* in thee.

And ye will find, as the days come, as the weeks pass, that ye will be shown from day to day the next step. For He is thy God and thy counsel, and thy help, and upon His arm may ye lean; upon His hand may ye be led in the things, the experiences, the conditions through which ye may pass.

[Background: Engineer, educator, manufacturer, Protestant. He sought advice on establishing a boys' school and on problems concerning getting it started. He was also interested in how he could be more helpful to the Cayce work.]

Reading 165-26

(Q) How can entity make himself more fit for this work?

(A) Look within, and rely more upon that promise—yea, the many promises of Him who is Life and Strength—yea, the very salvation of a sin-sick world!

Do not confuse self, do not overstep self, but as hath been said, "When ye call I will *hear*—and answer speedily."

This applies to thee—yea, to each soul, to be sure; but make it thine own cry, *with* the *willingness* in self to be led, to be guided, to be directed, by that as *He* hath given, "Ask in my name and ye—believing—shall have."

Can there be a greater promise? Oft ye, as so many, feel—or act—as if this meant someone else.

Is not thy soul as precious in His sight as though ye had taken a city, yea as though ye had directed a nation?

For ye are gods in thine own making, if ye hold to Him. Not in self, as of self's disappointment. Know that disappointment is with Him, and He is just as hurt. But be ye rather joyous that ye are counted worthy to be a channel, an opportunity, through which even one soul may find the way.

For he that hath saved a soul hath indeed covered a multitude of shortcomings!

In such meditation, then—in such may the self awaken to that strength of purpose, that *determination* to *carry on!* Though the world forsake thee, if thy Lord is upon thy side, ye stand even as Eleazar before the hosts of the Lord. [Num. 3:32]

But whom the Lord would exalt, He first brings low that they may know the strength is of the Lord—and not in hosts but the still small voice that beareth witness with thy soul, thy spirit, that ye walk that straight and narrow way that leadeth to understanding. And in saving those of thy own shortcomings, ye find ye have been lifted up.

[Background: Real estate broker, Quaker, spiritualist. This was a life reading.]

Reading 1646-2

Oft the entity becomes, or is considered by others as being, "heady," or head-minded, or bull-headed—as some would say, to give it an expressive feeling or emotion.

These are a part of the entity's experience. As to whether or not such urges become material manifestations depends upon the manner in which the will entertains such within the experience of the entity, or how those opportunities are used that may be given for the expression of such, by the associations of the entity in the material sojourns in relationships to others.

For, will is that factor in the experience of each entity in material manifestation which gives the ability to choose that as may be for the development or the retardment. For, as has so oft been indicated, there is today—now—set before each and every entity, every soul, that which is life and death, good and evil. Each entity, each soul, chooses in its manifestations. Because of urges latent or manifested, it is the expression of the *will* of the entity.

Thus, as there is expressed less and less of self, and more of an ideal as may be found in Him—who is the way, the truth and the life—in the relationships one to another, whether in the mental or material experience—there becomes the developing of an individual entity.

Then, latently, these as urges are those things with which the entity here has to reckon. What ye will do about them depends upon what is thy ideal—not an ideal in the material alone, nor mental alone; but as the entity finds self manifesting mentally, spiritually, physically, with choices to be made in each phase, so there must be the ideal of the experience in each phase—not merely idealistic, nor merely form.

For, as will be seen from other experiences and sojourns, such expressions are inclined to take the place of the real activity in the experience of the entity. *Form* alone has its influence, but it may be merely the shadow of that which is real.

For in the same manner ye mete to thy brother day by day, ye meter to thy Maker. For, "Inasmuch as ye do it unto the least of my brethren, ye do it unto me" said He—that is the truth, the way, the life . . .

As to the abilities of the entity in the present, and that to which it may attain, and how:

First, analyze thyself. What is thy ideal?

Then, study to show thyself approved unto God, a workman not ashamed, rightly dividing the words of truth, and keeping self unspotted from condemnation on thine own part—or from others.

Let not thy good be evilspoken of. Do all things in decency and in order, creating about thee the creative influences—not only through thy words but rather by what ye *are* day by day! For what ye are speaks so loud, seldom is what ye say heard by thy fellow man!

As ye would that others should do to you, do ye even so to them.

[Background: Writer, radio broadcaster, Protestant. This was a follow-up life reading in which Cayce counseled her on how to use her talents and abilities for her highest development and service.]

Reading 1472-3

For, as then, the evolution of man's experiences is for the individual purpose of becoming more and more acquainted with those activities in the relationships with the fellow man, as an exemplification, as a manifestation of Divine Love—as was shown by the Son of man, Jesus; that *each* and every soul *must become, must be*, the *savior* of some soul! to even *comprehend* the purpose of the entrance of the Son *into* the earth— that man might have the closer walk with, yea the open door to, the very heart of the living God . . .

(Q) *How can I extend the scope of my writing opportunity to use this ability in more important channels and wider service than at present?*

(A) As may be gathered from that as given, by putting into first thine own experience, thine own activity, those teachings of Him; not as tenets but as *living* experiences! So manifesting same in the lives and minds of those whom the self may meet day by day, learning that lesson as He so well manifested, that it was not in the separation as John, not in the running away as Elijah, not as in sitting in high places as Isaiah, not as in that form of Jeremiah—mourning; not in that lording as Moses—but *all things unto all men!* reaching them in their own plane of experience; and not with long-facedness!

For as He—He wined, He dined with the rich, He consorted with the poor, He entered the temple on state occasions; yea He slept in the field with the shepherds, yea He walked by the seashore with the throngs, He preached to those in the mount—*all things*; and yet ever ready to present the tenets, the truths, even in those forms of tales, yea parables, yea activities that took hold upon the *lives of men and women* in *every* walk of human experience!

So ye will find that the lessons ye gave then may be used today! Why? Because Truth is *truth, ever*—in *whatever stage*, in whatever realm of evolution, in *whatever* realm ye find same; it is as He gave—the little leaven.

Think not, even as He, to do some great deed that would make the welkin ring throughout the earth. Rather *know* it is the little line, the little precept, the little lesson given into the lives and experiences that brings the awareness into the hearts and souls of men and women; that consciousness of the *nearness* in the still small voice within.

For as proclaimed of old, it is not in the thunder or lightning, it is not in the storm, it is not in the loudness—but the still small voice within!

So as ye write, so as ye talk, so as ye love—let it be in meekness of spirit, in *purposefulness* of service, in an activity and an eye single to the *glory* of the Father through those that are His children.

For "Who is my mother, my brother, my sister? They that do the will of the Father, the same is my mother, my brother, my sister."

What is the will? Love the Lord with all thy heart, thy mind, thy body; thy neighbor as thyself!

Sow the seeds of kindness, helpfulness, longsuffering, gentleness, patience, brotherly love; and leave the *increase* to the Father, who *alone* can give same either in the spirit, the mind *or* the body!

Being patient even as He.

4

●

Application in Daily Life, with Jesus as the Pattern

[Background: Retired banker, Quaker, Protestant. He had expressed an interest in studying "the nature and laws of Spirit." This was a mental-spiritual reading in which he sought advice on devoting himself to spiritual healing and the reinforcement of his physical and mental powers.]

Reading 1662-1

EC: Yes, we have the body, the enquiring mind; and those conditions physical, mental and spiritual as relate to this body's activity in this material experience.

Much may be given respecting the choice, the desire of the body in its willingness to be a channel through which greater spiritual enlightenment may come.

It is a choice that is well for the entity, for the body; for the peace and harmony that such may bring into the experience of the entity.

Then, we would approach each phase from its own activity and relationship.

As is understood by the entity, each must coordinate—one with another.

Then, in the practice and in the application of the fruit of the spirit we find that the desire and the purpose may be made a practical experience for the entity in its activities among its fellow men.

First—the physical body is the temple, the encasement of the mind and soul of the entity. It has its virtues, its faults, its weaknesses, its strengths. Yet, as is understood, he that is wholly—mentally, spiritually, in accord with the oneness of the Christ Consciousness may expect and may live and may know within self the *proper* course for the activities to bring the best welfare for the body.

But that these may be fortified, that the mental self may be assured—we will point out the weaknesses, and how—materially, mentally—these may be strengthened that the higher spiritual and mental self may have then the better, the greater channel through which to magnify the spirit of truth that may indeed set not only self but others *free* in this material experience.

There are deficiencies in the blood supply in giving sufficient of energy for the physical being.

Each of these phases must be met in its own scope and sphere of activity.

Then, by following nature's courses—in that as there is given the mental body to feed upon, this or that spiritual or natural law, so does it apply same in its relationships to self as to others; also the material or natural laws respecting the physical body.

Keep same then clear, clean from those defects or deficiencies that would hinder in the natural processes of resuscitating and reviving its own self; supplying sufficient of energies; keeping a balance between the natural salts of the body itself so that the chemical reaction within same is purified.

Thus, not such a diet as to be contrary to natural laws, but that which is in keeping with the manner in which the body exerts self—so that there may be brought the better resuscitating influences and forces.

Upon the natural things, then, that replenish and supply energies—as in these; not as the only things eaten, but this as an outline for the activities of the body to preserve and maintain a balance:

Mornings—the natural answer to the call for the foods that supply the body; such as whole wheat, whole rye—either in their combinations or separately, but in their natural state or natural sources. Eggs. Fruits. All of these in their regular season are to be a portion of the diet; not as a conglomerate mass, not as combining cereals at the same meal with fruits—for these defeat then their purposes. Then when fruits are taken, do not take the cereals. When the cereals are taken, leave off the fruits.

Noons—a portion of this meal should be of raw vegetables.

Evenings—have the special or regular vegetables carrying the activities so needed, preferably cooked in their *own* salts rather than combined with other things—or such combinations as to be at variance one with another.

Little of meats, but when these are taken we find that fish, fowl or lamb would be preferable. Never fried foods.

Have sufficient activity between the meals so that the bodily energies have sufficient exercise to keep a normal balance, thus using up the energies as created by that which has been taken into the system for activity.

Do these, combining same with the seeking as would be a part of the regular activity to keep and maintain and build a better resistance in the influence of the physical forces of the body—in these activities through this material experience.

Then, for the body-physical-mental self—the Mind is the Builder. The attitude individuals maintain, as an entity, towards conditions, individuals and activities, creates that atmosphere for the supplying of energies from that which has been taken as the material for supplying the physical body.

Thusly: If one partakes of the fruit of the vine, or of cereal or of what not, and then holds the attitude of fire or *resentment* or animosity or hate—what can the spiritual and mental self do with such an attitude in those environs created by the attitude for such an assimilation or digestion in a body active in material forces!

Thus, as has been indicated, what would be the practical application of the mental self respecting conditions, individuals, influences about it of every nature!

First—patience, love, longsuffering, gentleness, kindness; speaking not of anyone in a resenting manner. For know, as He hath given, all power that is in the influence of an individual, a nation, a country, is only lent of the Lord as an opportunity for the individual according to that it has once purposed—or to carry forward that He hath willed respecting each soul!

For ye know, ye understand—all stand as one before Him. There are no ones above another; only those that do His will. What is His will? "Thou shalt love the Lord with all thy heart, thy mind, thy body—and thy neighbor as thyself." This is the whole law—the spiritual law, the mental law, the material law. And as ye apply same, thus ye become the *law!* For as He, thy Master, thy Lord, thy Christ fulfilled the law by compliance with same, He became the law and thus thy Savior, thy Brother, thy Christ! for in Him ye find, ye see the example that is set before thee pertaining to the natural life, the mental life, the material life, the spiritual life. Not an extremist, and not a conservative—but one who met each experience in a manner in which there was *never* a question in His Consciousness as to its purpose, His desire and the ability to be one with the purpose of the Creative Force—God!

Thus, as He is the water of life, as He is the bread of life, as He is the vine, as He is the sower—so in Him ye see, ye find thy example!

What then are His promises to thee? What relationship beareth He to thee? Thy Brother, thy Guide, thy Savior! For He took upon Himself the burden of all. And as ye read, as ye interpret the 14th, 15th, 16th and 17th of John, know that these are to thee—not to just anyone, but to *all*— "whosoever loveth me and keepeth my commandments, to him will I come—and I will abide with him."

These are thy promises. Thus as He may act through thee in thy physical, thy mental preparation of thy body—which has been and is lent thee, thyself, thy entity, thy soul—ye may be the channel. For as He gave, "Inasmuch as ye do it unto the least of these, my children, ye do it unto me."

Then oft in thy spiritual meditation enter into the holy of holies with Him, for there He hath promised to meet thee. For "if ye will open the door, I will enter and sup with thee." This is thy promise, this is *thine*— "that ye may be glorified in me," saith He, "as I may be glorified in the Father." And thus is the love of the Father for His children fulfilled in thy activity.

These do not become then theory—they do not become speculative; but as ye do them, so is it measured to thee again. For greater love hath no man than that he lay down his own self for those that he loves. And that alone that ye give, have given—of thy body, thy mind, thy strength—do ye possess. Just as He—as thy Guide, thy Guard, thy *hope*—has given Himself; so are ye His.

So as ye expend your body, your mind, your purposes, your desires, to bring to others the consciousness of His abiding presence, so may ye *know* His peace, so it may be thine as ye accept, as ye use, as ye apply same in thy relationships to thy fellow man day by day.

For as He hath given, God hath not willed that any soul should perish but hath with every temptation prepared a way, a manner through which the knowledge of His love, of His promises, may come to the consciousness of His children.

That thy choice has been and is to be used in a service of bringing healing to those that are without hope, that are in the throes of fear and doubt, is a *noble* purpose, a noble desire! And His blessings, His promises *will abide with thee* as ye abide in His love day by day!

It is not, then, any great influence or force that may be set as to cause the welkin to ring. It is not with the sound of trumpet, nor with the shouting—but rather the still small voice within that brings the assurance to thee that thou art His and He is thine.

For as He gave, "My Spirit beareth witness with thy spirit." And behold, He hath given His angels charge over thee, and they stand ever—as He—before the throne of grace and mercy, lest thou find thyself alone and doubt also.

But only as ye keep thy face towards His are His promises sure in thee.

Then, ye ask: What is the manner of procedure for the entity, for the assurance that thou art His and that ye have been indeed called!

As indicated, first—keep thy temple, thy body, in accord with the natural laws; that ye may keep that health, physically, that ye would give to others. And that ye give is not of thyself but of Him. For He is life. Life itself, then, in all its forms, its phases, is a manifestation of Him, the Maker, the Creator of all that is!

For as given of old, He is the Word—and He dwelt among men. And He became manifest to men.

So may He—in thy work, in thy prayer, in thy meditation, in thy *treatment* of thy fellow men day by day—become manifest in their lives. For He increaseth in power, in might, as *ye* pour Him out in thy love for thy fellow man! by practicing, daily, the fruits of the spirit!

Sow, then, the seed of same; leaving the results, leaving the increase to Him alone who may increase same.

Then not of thyself but that His power of the Christ, working in and through thee, may bring not only health but peace—and such peace as He promised; not as the world knoweth peace but as only those who walk and talk oft with their God!

Well hast thou chosen! *Well*-equipped thou may be; putting on then the whole armor of love, of faith, of hope, of charity. Thus may ye fill that place, that purpose for which ye came into the experience in this earth.

Let love, then, be without dissimulation. Abhor that which is evil. Cleave to that which is good—even as He. For He looked not upon men because of their estate but rather "who is my brother? who is my mother, my father? they that do the will of the Father, the same is my mother, my brother, my sister."

So as ye manifest in thy dealings with thy fellow man the fruits of the Spirit, thus do ye become physically, mentally, spiritually equipped for the kingdom of righteousness—which must be within!

Ready for questions. (No questions)

Now—may the blessings of Him who is able to keep thee, rest and abide with thee through the love as is promised thee in Him, Jesus the Christ!

Amen!

We are through for the present.

[Background: Office worker. This reading was sought to clarify and expand on a life reading she had previously received and to advise her on how to make practical use of it in her daily life.]

Reading 524–2

In applying, then, that which has been given, first analyze self, self's impulses, self's innate desires, self's inhibitions, self's aspirations; and it may be seen—as these are put into the same form or manner—how or *why* these conditions, experiences, desires, wishes, have arisen in the experience of the body.

Where there has been the application in the past or in the present experience of those laws—and loves—that pertain to that which is constructive or in keeping with that set as the ideal in the spiritual expressions in material manifestations, there has been growth. Where there has been desire or the application of self in those things or conditions whereunto the developments were for the satisfying or gratifying of self's own interest alone, or for the aggrandizement of self, this has made rather for retardments—or meeting in the varied manners and experiences, as has been seen in the present, as has been pointed out in those activities in the past—that have brought to the material manifested forms consternation, disorder, distrust, or those things that are not of the spirit.

For, as has been oft given, there has been a standard, a measuring stick whereunto any soul may measure itself as He has given: "As oft as ye do it unto the least of these, my brethren, ye do it unto me." And, "Many shall come in that day saying, In thy name we cast out demons, healed the sick, and yet I will say I never knew you." For those that have applied even those in the light of self's own interest have their reward already. They that have ministered that the God-force, the soul that is the image of the Maker *might* be glorified have done so unto the Lord. His brethren, His individual selves are but the material manifestations of that Creative Force in a material world. Then, in making the application of self in those fields of activity that have been pointed out whether in the home, in the street, in the market place, or in associations with the individuals in their various walks of life, these are but the channels or the places or the experiences or the opportunities whereunto there may be the application of that which has been given as the whole law and the prophets: "Ye shall love the Lord thy God with all thine heart, thine soul, thine body, and thy neighbor as thyself."

In this manner may there be the practical application of those things given, that the soul, the heart, the mind, may grow in grace, in knowledge, in understanding, and *thus* create for self and the associations and the surroundings that first of contentment, then peace and harmony that will make for the more and more awareness of His presence abiding with thee . . .

(Q) How may the material activities and the spiritual purpose be coordinated?

(A) That in the material world is a shadow of that in the celestial or spiritual world. Then, the material manifestations of spiritual impulse or activity must be in keeping or in attune with that which has its inception in *spiritual* things. For, the *mind* of man *is* the builder; and if the beginning is in spiritual life, and the mental body sees, acts upon, is motivated only by the spiritual, then the physical result will be in keeping with that thou hast sown. For, what ye sow ye shall reap, and God is not mocked; for the desire, the intent and purpose must be toward that first law as given: "Thou shalt have no other gods before me. Thou shalt love the Lord thy God with all thine heart, thine soul, thine body." If the activities make for the exaltation of the mind, the body, or the position, power, wealth or fame, *these* are of the earth earthy. Not that there should not be the material things, but the result of spiritual activity—*not* the result of the desires for that which the material things bring *as* power to a soul . . .

(Q) *What is the lesson that may be drawn from my entrance into the present plane?*

(A) That purpose for which the soul entered in, under those circumstances and conditions in the earth's experience in the present, that the soul might meet in this experience that which will make for the more sureness in Him. For, the earth is His and the fullness thereof. For, as given, God and the Christ Spirit is Life itself; and the motivating force of the soul is either for that companionship, that association, that development which will make such a soul–body as a fit companion for that Creative Influence manifested in the earth in Him, or it is for separating self from Him. For, in the Beginning was the Word, and that Spirit, that Christ Spirit *was* the Word. That Word was made flesh, even as each soul that manifests in the earth is made flesh. That soul, that spirit, *dwelt* among men, and that soul made itself of no estate; yet the Creator, the Maker, the Giver of the life itself; that man, that each soul, that this soul, might know that it has an advocate *with* the Father through Him that gave Himself as a ransom. How? For, as the impulses in self arise, know those impulses have arisen in Him; yet through the ability to overcome death in the material world is His presence able to abide with thee, dost thou trust in Him and not in self. Or, as He gave, in Him who *is* the Maker and the Creator is life alone, and they that put their trust in anything else climb up some other way. But they that put their trust in Him are His, and He calleth them by name, and He abideth with them. When ye call on Him He is very near.

Know, then, that in this experience thou mayest come to know Him as thine daily companion in whatsoever thou doest; for, "If ye love me, keep my commandments." What are His commandments? A new commandment He gave, that ye love one another, even as He hast loved thee.

[Background: Electrical engineering student. This was a mental and spiritual reading in which he had asked about the soul's purpose for entering into the earth.]

Reading 440–4

As to the purposes, then, for the soul's forces entering into matter in the beginning: That there might be a comprehending of how material forces acted upon spiritual, or *spirit*, endeavor of an entity, a soul. For, here we would give the variation between the mental mind of an earth being and the spirit that occupies its space in that man calls space. For, it must be learned or comprehended within thine consciousness as a being, in a finite force of activity, that time and space are one; and the divisions of these have been set in human experience and human endeavor that there might be the destruction of the physical forces that the spiritual might catch here a line, there a line, here a precept, there a precept, that there might be gained more and more that consciousness that is sought by the inmost recesses of this entity's desire, and again lived in the present in such a way and manner that the fruits of the spirit may be in thine own consciousness. For, self must become selfless, and the spirit must become magnified in the relationships of the individual's activity in its meeting with the fellow man; whether this is in relationship to seeking to know how the response of spirit or spirituality in the experience of another soul acts upon it in its environ, in its surrounding, in its journey back to its Creator, or what not. For, as given of old (and let these be not as platitudes in thine own experience), as a man, as a heart, as an experience is sown, so shall the harvest be, according to the application of those things that make for growth in the realm of that sought. For, to say "Do good" unto thy neighbor and then stand aside and see what will happen when others act in this or that way and manner does not bring an experience to self; for only through experience may the soul, the mind, the heart, the body, become aware of the effect of any application of the law of continuity of force, continuity of life, or of forces that make for growth in the experience of a soul.

Then, know: As ye sow, so shall ye reap. And in the material world there stands in the laws of the Creative Influences only these: "Thou shall love the Lord thy God with all thine heart, thine mind and thine soul," and the second is likened unto it: With the body and with the attributes of same, manifest to thine brother that law of God, and see in him—in thine brother, in the weakest among thine associates, in the weakest among thine companions—that spirit of God which if magnified will make for a growth of the *soul* in thine brother, that it may be found in the way that leads to life, to light, to immortality for that soul. And he that saves a soul has experienced, and does experience, that realm of joy, peace, solace, understanding, that may only come to those who have experienced in saving, in directing, in blessing, a soul. For, the soul of self, as the soul of thine brother, is seeking its way, its journey, to its Maker. The birthright of every soul, as given by its Creator is coming into a material plane, is the same as for self; that it may experience the fruits of the spirit that may be manifested in a manifestation of life in a material or earth plane . . .

In the application of self, then, as to the developments in the present experiences and in keeping that balance in body, in mind, in soul, in the activities of the self in this present sojourn, first seek to know self as to what is the impelling desire in thine inner self. Take counsel with soul, and let this be as thy first experience in thine psychic self; for psychic, as given, is but a name, yet its metes and bounds take hold upon the mental, the material and the spiritual things in the experience of every soul! But ask in self, "What *is* my purpose? What *is* my desire? Is it an experience that I may exalt my inner self? or that I may glorify my Maker, my Redeemer, my Lord, my Master?" And get the answer from the mental self! Then enter into meditation, in the wee hours of the morning, when the world at large is quiet—when the music of the spheres and the morning stars sing for the glory of the coming day, and ask the soul; and let the spirit of self answer. Audibly? Yea, within thine own heart will come the answer Yea or Nay.

Then, when thou hast made thine own skirts clear, thine own soul clean, until *He* answers within thee that thou, having chosen the better part, may be given the application or the privilege of using the talents thou hast developed in thine experiences. For, as indicated in that which has been meted or measured to thee, the purposes are well—if the intents are kept just as clean. For they would bring in the experience of thine brother, and thy neighbor, the more abundant life—and the more abundant understanding of the relationships of the creature to the Creator, and the *way* of the Creator with the creature. The Father hath given such a leeway to the sons of men that no force, no impelling force—unless sought or desired—and no activities in the material world, in the mental world, might be given. Then, if thine activities are such as to not belie that spoken in the mind or by the word of mouth, He will be thy guide—as thou wilt be His son.

Not that thine experience in the field of activity may be entirely different from that of thine next door neighbor, but find not fault in thine friend nor in thine enemy; for, hath not He, the Father, allowed the tares and the wheat to grow up together? Be not as one that would tell the Father, the Creator, as to who the tares are—or as to when such a tare should be rooted up. Be thou rather found in the way of *blooming*, of bringing forth fruit worthy of a son that has been endowed with the privileges of manifesting the spirit that He has shed abroad in the earth through the gift to the world of the Babe in Bethlehem, that grew in stature, in body, in mind, and then manifested the love of God in the way that He went about doing good to those that sought; yea, those that asked in the Father's name! For, ever were the blessings to the individuals in accordance to the desire of the soul.

Then, in applying self, my son, know that the Father liveth in thee, and will rightly guide thee in thy seeking and in thine steps day by day, if thou hast prepared His temple in thee for the place that He may abide. If thou keepest the temple cluttered up with those things that bespeak rather of the flesh, only the flesh can answer—but if thou keepest the temple clean and decorated in the spirit of love, and in the light of truth, then it will shed its light abroad, even as He has given, "I will not leave thee comfortless but will come and abide with thee, that ye may be my children and I will be your god."

Then, in seeking those things that will make for the greater understanding in thine present experience, let thy yeas be yea in the Lord, thy nays be nay in the Lord, and thy days will be long in the earth—and many will call thee blessed in His name; for the way is set before thee, and it is not past finding out. Doubt not, but seek. Seek in His name.

Ready for questions.

(Q) *What is the highest possible psychic realization—etc?*

(A) That God, the Father, speaks directly to the sons of men—even as He has promised.

[Background: This was a life reading in which the individual expressed an interest in reincarnation and psychic ability.]

Reading 707-1

From Venus and Uranus there are contradictory influences in the experience at times. Hence we find periods when the entity, through those activities and meditations in self, becomes wandering; losing that hold upon the strength that has raised, or that may—in its manifestations for its fellow man—become as a wonderment—and the entity doubts. Fears arise. If thou hast centered thy choice in self, be fearful! If thou art centering self in Him who has walked the way of men, Him who has known all the vicissitudes of an earthly experience in all its environs, whether in the dungeons of the earth, the slavedriven individuals or the leaders among men that would make war and love the flow of blood that that within themselves might be made glorified—if thou art centered in Him, then be *not* afraid! Yea, He has walked the streets with the rabble and has seen the flowing of the blessings that may come through making self humble! Yea, in the face and in the power of those that might save the body, He gave: "There is no power save that Creative Force we call God may give," that the soul may be raised, may be washed, may be white, may be cleansed that it may be in the presence of the Maker Himself! Art thou choosing this way? Thou knowest! Follow in His footsteps. Let Him ever speak, as He did to those

that were afraid; yea, though they had walked with the paths of understanding, though they had seen within themselves, yet when troubles
arose they became fearful within themselves. He gave that which is as
applicable today as it was from the beginning, "If ye will be my son, I
will be thy Father-God. If ye will trust in me, I will not forsake thee."
Though the heavens may fall, though the earth may pass away, thy
spirit and thy faith in Him will *not* be shaken, for He abides with thee
and hath given His angels charge concerning thee lest thou, in thy fury,
in thine self, dash thine head, thine foot, against the stone.

**[Background: Clerk, Protestant. This was a mental-spiritual reading. She
was concerned about her job and wondered if she should continue to
stay with the people she was living with or fulfill her dream of having a
home of her own.]**

Reading 357-13

Then, the more important, the most important experience of this or
any individual entity is to first know what *is* the ideal—spiritually.

Who and what is thy pattern?

Throughout the experience of man in the material world, at various
seasons and periods, teachers or "would be" teachers have come; setting
up certain forms or certain theories as to manners in which an individual shall control the appetites of the body or of the mind, so as to
attain to some particular phase of development.

There has also come a teacher who was bold enough to declare himself as the son of the living God. He set no rules of appetite. He set no
rules of ethics, other than "As ye would that men should do to you, do
ye even so to them," and to know "Inasmuch as ye do it unto the least of
these, thy brethren, ye do it unto thy Maker." He declared that the kingdom of heaven is within each individual entity's consciousness, to be
attained, to be aware of—through meditating upon the fact that God is
the Father of every soul.

Jesus, the Christ, is the mediator. And in Him, and in the study of His
examples in the earth, is *life*—and that ye may have it more abundantly.
He came to demonstrate, to manifest, to give life and light to all.

Here, then, ye find a friend, a brother, a companion. As He gave, "I call ye not servants, but brethren." For, as many as believe, to them He gives power to become the children of God, the Father; joint heirs with this Jesus, the Christ, in the knowledge and in the awareness of this presence abiding ever with those who set this ideal before them.

What, then, is this as an ideal?

As concerning thy fellow man, He gave, "As ye would that others do to you, do ye even so to them," take no thought, worry not, be not overanxious about the body. For He knoweth what ye have need of. In the place thou art, in the consciousness in which ye find yourself, is that which is *today, now,* needed for thy greater, thy better, thy more wonderful unfoldment.

But today *hear* His voice, "Come unto me, all that are weak or that are heavyladen, and I will give you rest from those worries, peace from those anxieties." For the Lord loveth those who put their trust *wholly* in Him.

This, then, is that attitude of mind that puts away hates, malice, anxiety, jealousy. And it creates in their stead, in that Mind is the Builder, the fruits of the spirit—love, patience, mercy, longsuffering, kindness, gentleness. And these—against such there is no law. They break down barriers, they bring peace and harmony, they bring the outlook upon life of not finding fault because someone "forgot," someone's judgment was bad, someone was selfish today. These ye can overlook, for so did He . . .

(Q) *Please give an affirmation that will help me.*

(A) In the terms of that indicated—as ye pray, in the morning, in the evening:

Here, Lord, am I. Use thou me, this day, this evening, as Thou seest I may serve others the better; that I may so live, O God, to the glory of Thy name, Thy son Jesus the Christ, and to the honor of mine own self in Thy name.

[Background: Student, Protestant. This was a life reading. The young man was about to be drafted and wondered whether to go back to Duke University.]

Reading 2549–1

For, know that each soul is a free–willed individual, and chooses the way and the application. For it is either the co-worker with God in

creation—and creative then in its attitude, in its thought, in its application of tenets and truths day by day; *or* in attune with that which is at
variance, and thus besetting or putting stumblingblocks in the way of
others along the way.

Each soul must choose of itself whom it will serve—self, the glorifying of same, fame or fortune as partakes of material things, or that
which is set in the Ideal Who thought it not robbery to make Himself
equal with God, but went about doing good—as ye have experienced,
as ye have seen.

Thus there is innately the soul's abilities to analyze conditions, manners, ways and means, but prompted ever by that which *is* the Way.

Thus there needs be no justification. For He, thy Lord, thy Master, has
justified thee before the Father.

Thus thy activity, thy choices in thy daily life should be to the *glorifying* of His purpose in the earth.

That is thy purpose. That ye must choose of thyself. For He inviteth
thee. For He hath given, "I stand at the door and knock; whosoever
openeth I will enter in and will abide with thee."

This then is not an idle promise, not something of long ago, not that
which is not thy very own—if ye will but accept same. For, "I will abide
with thee always" is to each soul. For man's advent into materiality is to
the glory of the Father.

**[Background: The 262 series of readings was given to the first Study
Group, whose purpose was to compile a work to spread the teachings
and philosophy of the readings to others. This particular reading dealt
with the first lesson, "Cooperation."]**

Reading 262-3

GC: You will have before you the group gathered here, and their
desire to be guided into the path of greater service through these forces;
together with that attempt of each throughout the week to gain through
meditation the data for the first lesson on cooperation. Please direct us
in the organization of this material, and give to each expansion and
interpretation of that received, as presented in questions from each.

EC: Yes, we have the group, as individuals, as a group, as gathered here. As they each seek in *their* way, through their development, to co-operate in being of service to others, so are they lifted up. As the consciousness of the Master is raised in their individual activities, so is the cooperation in a body as was from the beginning, when the cooperation brought into being those forces as manifest themselves in this material world. They each, then, keeping that creative force within themselves in that direction as makes for the continuity of life, hope, peace, understanding, so may it be builded in the lives of themselves first, then in others—as *they*, in *their* way, seek to bring a better understanding in this material world.

Then, as ye are gathered here, let that mind [be in you] *not* of elementals, but of spiritual forces as may come *through* thine efforts if they are made in accord with His will. Let thy prayer be continually:

Not my will but Thine, O Lord, be done in and through me. Let me ever be a channel of blessings, today, now, to those that I contact, in every way. Let my going in, mine coming out be in accord with that Thou would have me do, and as the call comes, "Here am I, send me, use me!"

Ready for questions.

(Q) [307]: *How may we have the mind of Christ?*

(A) As we open our hearts, our minds, our souls, that we may be a channel of blessings to others, so we have the mind of the Christ, who took upon Himself the burden of the world. So may we, in our *own* little sphere, take upon ourselves the burdens of the world. The *joy*, the peace, the happiness, that may be ours is in *doing* for the *other* fellow. For, gaining an understanding of the laws as pertain to right living in all its phases makes the mind in attune with *Creative* Forces, which *are* of *His* consciousness. So we may have *that* consciousness, by putting into action *that* we know . . .

(Q) [311]: *How may I best cooperate with and serve this group?*

(A) Do with all thy might what thy hand finds to do. Let *this* mind be in you as was in Him, "Not as I will but *thine* will be done in earth as it is in heaven." Make thine self a channel of blessings to *someone*; so will His blessings come to thee, as an individual, as an integral part of the group. "They that seek my face shall find it."

82   Jesus as a Pattern

[Background: From the 262 series, this particular reading dealt with the lesson "Wisdom."]

Reading 262–105

GC: You will have before you Norfolk Study Group #1, members of which are present here, and work on the present lesson, copy of which I hold in my hand. You will continue the discourse on the lesson Wisdom.

EC: Yes, we have the group as gathered here; as a group, as individuals, and their work upon the lesson Wisdom.

In continuing with the discussion upon the Wisdom of the Father, let first each of you attune yourselves to that consciousness as may be had through attuning self in this meditation:

Our Father who art in the heaven of our own consciousness, so attune my mind, my body, with the infinite love Thou hast shown to the children of men, that I in body, in mind, may know the Wisdom of the Father in Jesus, the Christ.

Then it behooves each to be more aware of that love as brings into the experience of each soul the understanding that we as individuals cannot bear the cross of life alone but that the Father in His Wisdom has given to each an ensample, a promise to the children of men—"which is indeed mine now if I will but choose the love of Jesus in my daily life, in my walks among my fellow men."

In Wisdom thou wilt not find fault. In Wisdom thou wilt not condemn any. In Wisdom thou wilt not cherish grudges. In Wisdom thou wilt love those, even those that despitefully use thee; even those that speak unkindly.

"In the Wisdom of Jesus do I claim the promises of God and know His Presence. Though in those things that are not always understood, it is His Wisdom that makes for the changing of the affairs of the material experiences, the environs, the opportunities for those who profess their faith to give of themselves in body, in mind, that they may indeed know the Wisdom of God in their experiences."

Know that the Wisdom of Jesus—that is the promise to all—is a part of the daily life, and not to be put on as a coat or a cloak but to be part and parcel of each and every entity.

This is the Wisdom to know, "As I purpose in my heart to do, it is in accord with that I profess with my mouth." It is Wisdom that the acts of the body, of the mind, be in accordance with that proclaimed to thy children, to thy neighbor, to thy friend, to thy foe.

For Life is in its material activity the Wisdom of the Father that men may everywhere manifest, that they—too—may be a part of the consciousness of the Cosmic Consciousness.

For as the ways of life become more complex individuals see rather the material than the mental and spiritual.

Yet to thee, to whom the Book of Life—yea, the record of thine experiences—has been opened, there is the awareness that ye are indeed the children of God. And as children in thy Wisdom ye may approach boldly the Throne of Mercy. For the prayers of the righteous are heard, for they have attuned in Wisdom to the God-Consciousness within, and have come to the realization that they are not alone but that He walketh and He talketh with those who have called upon His Name, and who day by day show forth in their conversation their love. For Jesus is the Way, Jesus is the Christ, Jesus is the Mediator, Jesus is Wisdom to those who will harken to do His biddings.

And as He hath given, "If ye love me, keep my commandments; for they are not grievous to bear. For I will bear them with thee, I will wipe away thy tears, I will comfort the brokenhearted, I will bring all to those in the ways that are in the Wisdom of God for thy expressions through each experience, in each activity of thine."

For thy soul in its Wisdom seeketh expression with Him. Smother it not in the doubts and the fears of materiality but in the spirit of love and truth that encompasseth all, and that is open to ye who have set thy hearts, thy faces, toward the love that is in Jesus, thy Friend, thy Brother.

These, my brethren—yea, these my beloved children—Know that in Him is the truth, the light. Ye have seen a great light. Ye have touched upon the Wisdom of the Father, as is shown in the Son.

Then make thy paths straight. Let thy conversation, thy wishes, thy desires be rather as one with Him who thought it not robbery to be equal with God.

Ye know the way. Do ye stumble in ignorance or in selfishness? Do ye doubt for the gratifying of thy body or for the fulfilling of the body-appetites?

Ye know the way. Let, then, that love of the Infinite fire thee to action, to *doing!* And indeed live as hath been shown.

Study to show thyself in body, in mind, approved unto that thou hast chosen in the words of Jesus thy Master, thy Brother—in dividing the words of life in such measures that all who know thee, yea that contact thee, take cognizance of the fact that thou walkest and thou talkest with Jesus day by day; keeping thyself in body, in mind, unspotted from the world.

This is the Wisdom of God and is thine if ye will but claim it as thine own.

And may the grace and the mercy and the peace of a life lived in thine own consciousness be thine through Him that is able to present our lives before the throne of God spotless, white as snow, washed in the blood of the sacrifices made in our own daily experience—even as He has shown us the way.

We are through.

[Background: Widow, writer, Protestant. This was a reading in which she sought counsel and guidance regarding her spiritual development and her life's work.]

Reading 1152–4

For remember first, God so loved the world as to give His Son that we *through* Him might know *life*—and in knowing it apply ourselves in such measures and manners as to become even as He, *living* examples, known of men; not of self but the Father, through the Son, working in us day by day.

As has been indicated then for the entity, this must and should grow more and more as a consciousness of the entity—the fact of the experiences of the mind and soul through those sojourns when there was caught the glimpse not only of God in Love manifested in the earth but the application of self in its relationships to the fellow man builded that experience into the soul such that there are the greater longings that find expressions in the desire for Creative Influences and Force; whether these find manifestations in conveniences for individuals or the home, or whether they find expressions in the desire for writing.

For those are the *mental* expressions—to arouse in the minds of others a desire for not merely self-expression but that self is more and more a channel through which truth and light and love and harmony and peace and mercy and grace and longsuffering may manifest.

These shall ever be the themes in the various manners of presenting whatever may be sought to be given. For the Mind is the Builder, and is both spiritual and very carnal.

If there is fed then to the mental forces, or upheld or picturized or visioned for the mind, that which builds a carnal force that is indeed of the earth-earthy, the expressions become then rather as in the slough of despair; for their fruit are but the smudges of light.

While if they are builded in hope and faith and charity and love, and patience, then indeed may the individual soul not only of self but to those to whom such may be given become aware that they, too, are a part of the Divine. And thus as He, show forth His love by just being kind and patient and longsuffering with those that one meets day by day.

Ready for questions.

(Q) *What am I here on earth for?*

(A) As just given . . .

And this *should* be the purpose of *any* and *every* entity or body that seeks to put before others the experiences of self as related to the dealings with the fellow man and the activity of spiritual purposes and spirituality in its application in the lives and experiences and associations of individuals.

For if the purpose is secular, if it is earthly, if it is for material gain, then ye already have thy reward. Is it not as the first law?

That these have not been accomplished and that there is apparently a standstill is because ye have failed to give the data *life!* Now ye have the consciousness of thy purpose *in* the experience, that there may be builded that consciousness in the lives of others through thy feeble efforts—though they to thee may be; yet know—as again is a first law—man may only sow the seed of life—God *alone* can give it life!

He giveth the increase! For He is the only source of life. Man may only, then, attune through self's experiences or self's interpretation, or self's understanding, to that which answers a call—or a chord within the rhapsody of the lives of others that brings into the consciousness the fact that God *is*, God *is*! And that Consciousness gives life and light. It is not what one believes but *who* one believes that counts! For as it was given, *know* in whom thou hast believed, and *know* He is able to keep that thou hast committed unto Him against any experience that may be thine in *thine* evolution or thy development, or thine activity in any sphere of experience.

[Background: Accountant, Protestant. This was a life reading. He wrote later that his reading was a milestone in his life.]

Reading 1650–1

These are immutable laws!

And as the individual entity practices, works at, does something *about* such, so does there come into the experience those things that make the vision broader, the purposes worthwhile, the desires holy.

Then ye begin to sow the seeds of the spirit in the mental attitudes and activities; which are: first, patience! For "In patience possess ye your souls!" In patience ye become aware that the body is but a temple, is but an outward appearance; that the mind and the soul are rather the furnishings, the fixings thereof, with which ye dwell, with which ye abide *constantly*!

And in patience, in brotherly love, in kindness, in gentleness, in those things that are of the Spirit, of the mental attitudes, ye will find the closer walks with the purpose of the material entering.

For each soul is in that process of development to become fully aware of its relationships to its Maker. And in the manifesting of the fruits of the Spirit ye find these are attitudes and activities towards thy fellowman, those ye meet day by day. And as thy Lord hath given, "In the manner ye do it unto the least of these ye meet day by day, so ye do it unto thy God."

What, then, is the purpose of the entering of a soul into material manifestations?

In the beginnings, or in the activities in which the soul manifested individually, it was for the purpose of becoming as a companion of

Creative Force or God; or becoming the whole body of God itself, with the ability—even as thy Pattern, as thy Savior, as thy Guide and Guard—to know thyself to *be* thyself, yet one with Him!

That is the purpose for each entering into the material activities.

5

●

Becoming Conscious of the Presence of Jesus the Pattern

[Background: Lawyer, Protestant. This was a mental and spiritual reading in which the individual expressed an interest in deep meditation.]

Reading 853–9

First, then, what is the ideal standard of an entity in the material plane? That which is of material success, fame or fortune, or what?

Are these (fame and fortune) the criterion by which judgements are drawn as to whether an individual has succeeded or not?

Hardly! For what is thy ideal as to the spiritual life? It is as the thought of every soul, that it, the soul, may know life in its broader sense. For it holds to that of continuity of self.

Then, the ideal that is in the heart of the individual, as here. For, as seen, what were the promptings in the experience of the entity to change from that of one in power among men, one feared, one dreaded; yet within the grasp or within hand that of power to rule men's lives by that of command, that of the specie that made for the medium of exchange as to worldly things?

Because the love divine, as was manifested in the man Jesus, was, is and ever will be the criterion of judgement upon the consciousness of an individual entity; yea, a personality, manifesting in the material world.

Then, judging as to this, we find that though He came in the flesh and was endowed by those who proclaimed Him with gold, frankincense and myrrh, He gave—the birds of the air have their nests, and the foxes have their holes or dens, yet the Son of man hath not where to lay his head.

Then life, and its experience in the material plane, cannot, must not, be made up only of that which causes men oft to forget their God, and their relationships to Him—and as to how these may be manifested in the earth.

Not that these things of the world do not have their place in the experience of each entity, yet these are the means to an end, and *not* the end.

For as He gave again, what profit it a man though he gain the whole world and has lost sight of being a soul?

Then the premise from which judgements may be drawn, and that from which the entity may know that there is soul development, there is the attunement of self with that consciousness that is the measure of standard, that is the bright and morning star, that is that rod of Jesse that still cannot be lost in the experiences of men:

That the love as was shown, as was manifested by Him, is *alone* the way, the manner in and through which the soul may become aware of its activity even in a sin-sick world.

For just being kind, just being gentle, is the means and the manner, the way. Not in a passive way, but even as He—who went about doing *good* each day.

Then, how may one know, how may one find that consciousness, that awareness of being One with Him—in Truth, and yet apply one's own physical attributes in the material world and not become material-minded?

How gave He as concerning this?

"Consider the lilies of the field, they toil not, neither do they spin; yet Solomon in all his glory was not arrayed like one of these."

How then are these sayings, these lessons of His, to be applied in the experience of the entity, [853]?

First study to show thyself approved unto Him, being not afraid but rightly dividing the words of truth; and keeping *self* unquestioned about the things of the world.

How does this then come in the experience of the entity in the present, for learning the deep meditation—and this ability to use that which is the birthright of each and every soul?

For the *soul*-entity is in the image of the Creator.

Then we find in the material body those patterns, those manners, those means. For indeed He hath given and has purposed that no soul shall lose its way, but He hath prepared for *every* soul the ways, the means of that soul knowing that He, Jesus, the Christ, is not only the Way but is the *directing* of the individual in the daily experiences—if you walk and talk with Him.

Then for what purpose is this communication, this development of the abilities of knowing that Jesus, the man—Christ, the Lord—is with thee day by day?

That ye may exalt thyself among thy fellowman? That ye may find the easy way in the daily experiences, and know nothing of the cries of thy fellowman—seeking, seeking—that cry aloud, and long, for the Way?

Was His way easy? Would ye be greater than thy Lord?

Ye may be equal with Him, for He hath given, "Abide in me and as I abide in the Father we may be one, that the *Lord* may be glorified in the earth."

Then if it is for self-gain, for self-exaltation, for the making of the way easy, ye seek that which may turn upon thee and destroy thy very activity.

But if it is that He may be glorified in thy fellowman, then ye may know.

For as He hath given, "If ye love me, keep my commandments; and as ye abide in me, ask and it shall be given thee the *desire of thy heart!*" If that desire is in accord, in attune, in at-onement with the constructive forces of thyself, thy experiences and thy relations. For He keepeth the way, ever.

Then as the body is the temple of the living soul, it is a part and parcel of the mind that is the builder.

Then as ye open in thy meditation, first surround thyself with the thought, the prayer, the desire that Jesus, in His promises, guide thee in thy seeking.

Then ye have set yourself aright.

Then again as ye raise thy power of vibratory forces through thy body, ye give thyself in body, in mind, in purpose, in desire, into the hands, into the keeping of His purposes with thee.

And His promises are sure; and that which ye receive, that *use!* For to have an ideal, for to have a purpose, for to have knowledge and understanding without the courage and the will to use same is to become a weakling, not worthy, not able above that doubt; even as Peter when he walked on the water.

And when you see the turmoils of the earth, and when you hear the cries of those that are fearful, and when you see the elements about thee apparently in destructive forces, and ye doubt—to be sure you sink into doubt and fear and despair; unless thy purpose is ever "Here am I, Lord, use me, direct me."

In that manner then, ye may attain to that consciousness of His presence, of His abiding with thee; that these influences may become the very forces that have been and are a portion of thine experience in the earth.

And when even thy fellows appear that were a part of thyself—what must ye do?

Preach and live Christ to them, in thy consciousness! Thus ye make *their* purpose, their desire, become that they, too, may know that which lifts thee above the herd and become as one that seeks to know His way!

Then, in thy material application, just make thy desire, thy purpose ever, one with Him.

Study then—not as by rote—that as begins like this: "I go to prepare a place for you, that where I am there ye may be also; for in my father's house are many mansions. Were it not so I would have told you. Ask and ye shall receive."

Study then, first, the 14th, 15th, 16th and 17th of John. *Apply* them, as "This is Jesus speaking to [853]—*speaking!*"

What is thy answer? "I am ready, Lord." Or, "As soon as I get this done, I'll try."

These ye must answer within thyself.

For the will of each entity, of each soul, is that which individualizes it, that makes it aware of itself; and as to how this is used makes thee indeed a child of God.

He hath not willed that ye should perish, that ye should want, that ye would not know Him. What have *ye* willed? What is thy way? What is thy desire?

It becomes then so simple that the simplicity becomes the complexness of the daily life.

Yet as ye enter into thy temple, where He hath promised to meet thee, *cleanse* thyself in body, in mind, in the manner as seemeth good to thee—whether washed with water, washed with blood, or with incense, or in music, or in the din of the city or in the quiet of the forest. For though ye take the wings of the morning and fly to the utmost parts of heaven, ye will find Him there; and though ye sink to the depths of hell ye will find Him there; and He hath promised, and as He hath given, "Though the heavens and the earth fail, and though they pass away, My word and my promise shall not pass away." And His promise has been, "When ye *call* I will *hear!*"

These are thine. These are thy possibilities, these are thy abilities. What will ye do with them?

[Background: From the 262 series, this particular reading dealt with the lesson "In His Presence."]

Reading 262-33

(Q) *Please expand on how we may prepare ourselves that we may abide in His presence.*

(A) This would refer rather to the individual experience; for in the preparations of self there are varied consciousnesses, and what to one might be necessary to another would be secondary, and to that which may be the attribute of good judgement, clean living, without thought of same being a command or a law of universal nature; yet as we, as individuals, become more and more conscious—through meditation and prayer, and *application* of that we seek in the way of preparation—of that which keeps or holds, or preserves us as individuals in the consciousness of His presence, we become more conscious of His presence abiding with us, as we let that mind—through meditation and prayer—

be in us during and at *all* periods.

Whether in joy, in sorrow, in trouble or in pain, let that mind be in you as was in He that gave, "I am with you *always* even unto the end of the world."

Will that consciousness of the Christ love make our joys the more joyous, our sorrows the more in accord with the manner in which He met sorrow, or disturbances in the material affairs more in accord with the manner in which *He* met the material conditions?

As individuals we oft find that that as He gave, in the "thought of the morrow," or "wherewithal shall ye be clothed" was meant for someone else; *not* us. That consciousness as He gave, "In patience possess ye your souls"; *what* becomes aware of His presence, the physical–carnal body or the spirit of life that impels the soul in its development?

Then, as His love is shed on us, as we muse and meditate and pray to that we hold as our door to His presence, do we become aware of, do we enter in, do we find ourselves abiding in His presence.

As we may experience by that abiding presence, what are the fruits of same? *Worries* pass away, joys take their place; for as He looked upon Peter in the hour of trial and of denial by him, who had been declared to be—that spoken by him—as the foundations of that He was to leave in the earth, did He frown or did He smile? What broke the heart of the man, the frown or the smile?

Then, when ye abide in His presence, though there may come the trials of every kind, though the tears may flow from the breaking up of the carnal forces within self, the spirit is made glad; even as He in the hour of trial, the hour of denial, *smiled* upon him and brought to re-membrance—even as He has said to each that has named the Name, "I will bring to remembrance the promises I have made, if ye will abide in my presence." The promises, then, are sure; and not a thing apart from those that abide in His presence, but are ever remembered in the hour not only of sorrow; not only is He the resurrection, not only is He to come in the hour of trial, but He supped also in the hours of joy with those in Cana, He enjoyed even the feast with Zaccheus, laughed and joked. "Yea, though I walk through the valley of the shadow of death— thou art with me; though I fly to the utmost parts of the heavens thou art with me." Will we, as individuals, then, know His presence? How? "If ye love me, keep my commandments." Are they then so burdensome, those commandments? What are His commandments? How may we abide—how may we show the love? "Inasmuch as ye have done it unto the least of these my little ones, ye have done it unto me."

Reading 2072–4

Then again the expression was in that entity as he entered through those channels indicated as necessary for the functioning of the material, mental and spiritual mind, for the advent of that influence manifested in what ye call the Christ Consciousness, the Christ awareness (Jeshua).

For, *this*—the Christ Consciousness—is the basis.

Thus, how may one combine all as may be there gathered, into the realm of activity in which the everyday individual is met? How may the entity apply self that there may be the broadening, the greater awareness of its purposes, its desires, its hopes?

The entity is ever surrounded with the guardian influences of that which has been created in self through the application of those laws for that manifestation being sought.

Then—what must be the attitude, what must be the activity?

Know that the entity has reached that period in its awareness when all must be in accord, coordinant with all forms of contact—in word, in speech, in daily application—that express those forces which are today a part of that group to which the entity may attain—through the activities in that realm, that state of consciousness, that state of awareness in this present experience.

Then, in summing up these:

The knowledge that there may be the greater expansion, the greater experience of enjoying here and now the satisfaction of knowing that the days are spent in the glorifying of the spirit of truth, makes and brings the awarenesses of every nature into the realm of the entity's consciousness.

For, He *is* thy guardian here and now. Put thy whole trust in those things indicated by Him, that ye have studied in this present experience: "As ye would that others should do to you, do ye even so to them."

Is this become trite? Too oft such is the reaction.

There may be the glimpses here and there, not only of the beauties but of the hardships, not only of the joys but of the besetting influences that make one afraid. In Him there was no fear. Of Himself little might have been accomplished in the earth, but being willing to be used He became the perfect channel. Be thou willing to be used in every form, as may be expressed in the very contrite manner, to love the Lord with all thy might, to encourage those who are weak, to assist those who seek to admonish and warn those who are of themselves self-sufficient in this material relationship.

These, then, are those forces, those characteristics and natures, those purposes made manifest that caused the kingdoms of the mental and spiritual realm—even of the earth—to be controlled by that influence which constantly lives those injunctions, "Be my people and I will be thy God."

Yes, there are the many approaches. There are the many awarenesses. Yet all that are of extremes, all that are of the contradictory notion to those that become the physical-minded, are manifested in Him.

"Be ye unafraid, for it is I."

That attitude, that purpose, that harmony should be and is the channel, the way that leads to the abilities for each soul to manifest the greater opportunity in the material experiences.

To love the Lord, then; to eschew evil, to keep from condemnation and to give blessings to all—that is the way, the truth in which the entity may make self fully aware of His walk with thee. Let not thy heart be troubled, neither let it be afraid; ye believe in God, believe also in Him— who went about doing good; knowing Himself, even as ye, to be a part of all that has been made manifest in the daily life.

These awarenesses bring greater abilities, greater harmonies into the experience. Hence they are the beauties—yea, the expressions of that rule and force and manner which should conduct the dealings of one entity with another, in those journeys along that way leading home!

Let that light, that harmony, that peace, take its time with thee. This brings the entity again to that second premise—as it, too, is a part of those awarenesses about the entity, of that love which makes itself manifest. For, if ye would have friends, ye must indeed show thyself friendly. If ye would know God and those relationships to Him, then, ye must seek after Him. For it is the answering of that spirit within thee to that spirit from which it comes.

Thus love thy neighbor as thyself. *Seek* to be that channel that causes those ye meet day by day to be better in every way because of coming in contact with thee; thinking better and better of themselves, by thy being less and less condemning of that about thee, or in thy relationships to things or peoples.

This too, then, becomes thy answer. Ye would love even as He hath loved thee. For it may become a living experience in thy own activity, in such measures as to bring not gratification of earthly things but attuning to that realm of the higher self which answers—"Thy spirit beareth witness with my spirit as to whether ye be the child of God or not."

These are the premises from which ye would judge or measure thyself. These are the rules, the regulations to be followed in humbleness of spirit, yet declaring day by day the mighty works of the living God as made manifest in the lives of those ye meet day by day in every way.

Let this prayer ever be that upon thy heart and mind, guiding thy purposes, thy hope offering: that ye may hold to that which is good, making same manifest by thought, by act, by purposes as to be one with Him.

[Background: Writer, Protestant. This was a mental-spiritual reading; she sought guidance in regard to psychic experiences, overcoming fear and doubt, and publishing her writings.]

Reading 2600-2

So the soul is that which is eternal.

Thus does there come in the experience of each soul those problems in a material world of the constant warring of material or changing things, or earthly experience, with mental and spiritual or soul forces.

The *way*, then, is that manifested in the Creative Force through Jesus, the Christ, the Son; for He is the way, the truth, the light in which the body, the mind, the soul may find that security, that understanding, that comprehending of the oneness *of* the spiritual with the material that is manifested in an individual entity.

To this entity, problems arise in the body-forces. While the mind is in attune, the soul is in an at-onement, the physical conditions to the entity become as stumblingblocks.

Remember rather the pattern as was manifested for thee in the Son; how that though He were the Son, yet learned He obedience through the things which He suffered.

He used, then, that which was necessary in the experience in the earth as periods of suffering, as periods of rejection, even by His own that He had called, that were His friends; not as stumblingstones but as steppingstones to make for thee, for the world, that access for each soul, for the closer relationship of the Father, through the Son, to the children of men.

This is thy heritage, then; not as one that knows not, but as one being reminded—put on the whole armor. Fret not at those things that may appear to hinder, but let that harmony as thou hast expressed, as thou may express to others, be in such measures as to bring—even as He— that hope, that light, that peace which comes from the closer walk with Him day by day.

Let thy prayer be, ever—*Here am I, Lord: Use me, in that way, in that manner Thou seest fit: Not my will but Thine, O God, be done in me, through me, day by day. May my going in, my coming out, be always acceptable in thy sight* . . .

(Q) *How can I obtain relief from resentment and bitterness?*

(A) As ye forgive, ye are forgiven. As ye love, so are ye loved. As ye resent, so are ye resented. This is *law*—physical, mental and *spiritual!*

Then, chuck it out of thy life. Let the love of God so fill thy mind, thy body, that there is *no* resentment.

As to how—though ye may not of thyself, put the burden on Him and it becomes light. But *act* in the manner as He did, not resenting any. For remember, as He said to that one who had promised that though all might forsake Him, he never would, yet in the same hour denied that he ever knew Him—"When thou art converted, strengthen thy brethren." Thus may it be given to thee—if ye put that resentment away, if ye put that doubt and that fear upon Him, He will cast it out; but thee, strengthen thy brethren. Teach, preach, talk to others, as to how they should leave such at the Cross and *only* magnify, manifest, *know* that they need not attempt to justify themselves. For, *all* the justification is in Him. We need then only to *glorify* that love, that hope, that understanding which He brings to each soul that seeks His face.

[Background: This was among a series of readings given on the topic of Jesus. This particular reading was given to the prayer group that worked with the Cayce information—"the Glad Helpers."]

Reading 5749–10

Then may ye as seekers of the way, may ye that have come seeking to know, to experience, to *feel* that presence of the Christ Consciousness within thine own breast, within thine own experience, *open* the door of thy heart!

For He stands ready to enter, to those who will bid Him enter.

He comes not unbidden, but as ye seek ye find; as ye knock it is opened. As ye live the life is the awareness of His closeness, of His presence, thine.

Then, again as He gave, "Love ye one another," thus fulfilling *all* that is in the purpose of His entrance into materiality; to replace hate and jealousy and those things that make one afraid, with love and hope and joy.

So be ye then as His children—those that show joy and gladness in the lives, the experiences, the hearts, the minds of those ye meet day by day; thus becoming indeed brethren with Him, in that He gave Himself as a ransom for all, that whosoever will may take *their* cross and *through* Him know the joy of entering into that realm of replacing jealousy and hate and selfishness with love and with joy and with gladness.

Be ye glad. Be ye joyous when those things come to be thy lot that should or would disturb the material-minded. Like Him, look up, lift up thy heart, thy mind unto the Giver of all good and perfect gifts; and cry aloud even as He, "My God, my God! Be Thou near unto me!"

In this, as ye raise then thy voice to Him, ye may be sure He will answer, "Here am I—be not afraid. For as the Father hath sent me, so come I into thy heart and life to bring gladness, that there may be life more abundant in thy experience."

Then, be ye *glad* in Him.

[Background: Writer, Catholic. This was a mental and spiritual reading in regard to his life and work. He later became a successful author but was plagued for years with crippling illnesses.]

Reading 849-11

In giving that as we find that may be helpful to the entity at this time, know that thou hast chosen well in thine mental and spiritual activities in the present. Hold fast to that faith exemplified in thy meditation, in thy counsels, in thy giving out to thy fellow man. For he that hides himself in the service of his fellow man through the gifts, through the promises as are in Him, hides many of those faults that have made afraid through the experiences in the earth. For as has been oft given, it is not what one knows as knowledge that counts, nor what one would attain in the material realms, but what one does about that which is known respecting constructive forces and influences in the experiences of the self and the fellow man. For as He hath given, "As ye do it unto others, ye do it unto me." *He is* the way, the life, the light. He *is* the Creator; He *is* the Giver of all good and perfect gifts. Man may sow, man may act in the material manifestations of the spiritual forces that move in matter; yet the returns, the increase, must come from and through Him that *is* the gift of life. It is not a consideration as to where or even how the seed of truth in Him is sown; for *He* gives the increase if it is sown in humbleness of spirit, in sincerity of purpose, with an eye-single that He may be glorified in and among thy fellow man. *This* is the way; this is the manner that *He* would have thee go.

Let thyself, then, become more and more a channel through which *His* manifestations in the earth may arise through thy efforts in the hearts, the minds of thy fellow man. For Mind (in man, to man) is the Builder, ever. That, then, must be directed, given, lost in singleness of purpose, that there may come the greater awakening within the consciousness of thy fellow man that He *is* in the earth; that His words are as the lights to men in dark places, to those that are weak, to those that do stumble. For He will give thy efforts that necessary force, that necessary power, to quicken even those that are asleep in their own selfishness, in their own self-indulgence, and bring to their awakening that which will make for the glorious activities in the earth.

Keep, then, the faith thou hast had in Him; for He is thy strength, He is thy bulwark, He is thy Elder Brother. To Him, *in* Him, ye may find that which will bring to thee alone—joy, peace, happiness, and that which makes me not afraid. For He *is* peace; not as men count peace, not as men count happiness, but in that harmonious manner in which life, the expression of the Father in the earth, *is one*—even as He is *one* . . .

For what is Destiny? The destiny of every soul is in *Him* who gave the soul, that the entity, the individual, might know, might be one with that Creative Force we call God. And how, the manner in which the entity, the individual, uses the opportunities makes for whether there comes the consternation, the turmoils, the strifes that arise from self-exaltation, or just the opposite. For how hast thy God meted to thee judgements? Not other than in mercy as thou showest mercy, as thou art a portion of that. What *will* ye do with this man thy elder brother, thy Christ, who—that thy Destiny might be sure in Him—has shown thee the more excellent way. Not in mighty deeds of valor, not in the exaltation of thy knowledge or thy power; but in the gentleness of the things of the spirit: Love, kindness, longsuffering, patience; these thy brother hath shown thee that thou, applying them in thy associations with thy fellow man day by day, here a little, there a little, may become one with Him as He has *destined* that thou shouldst be! Wilt thou separate thyself? For there be nothing in heaven, in earth, in hell, that may separate thee from the love of thy God, of thy brother, save thine own self!

[Background: Protestant, schoolteacher. In this reading, she sought help to enable her to reach the Christ Consciousness.]

Reading 272-9

In seeking that which may be helpful to the body-mind and body-consciousness in the present, well that the entity review in part much that has been given and that has been learned by the body.

The man, the body, and the manifestations of the flesh are as but a channel, a manner, a means through which the soul may through its activities manifest the attributes of the spirit of truth. Man finds himself in that state where he is subject to the faults, the failures, those conditions that work upon the weaknesses wherein he has failed. And, as an individual finds, these work through environmental and hereditary in-fluences, also through associations. Yet there is ever the awareness in the experiences of those who seek, that the Father, the God, the Creative Force, has prepared—has given man, the individual—the way of escape from those things that so easily beset. That the activities must become the voluntary choice of the entity, the soul, has been shown, mani-fested, given in the manner in which the Christ Consciousness in the earth was manifested through the lowly Nazarene; that came in order that man—through His example, His love, His patience, His hope mani-fested, through the attributes of the Spirit that He exemplified in His activity both as to word and as to precept—might choose, as He, to do that which is right, that which is just, that which is sincere, that which is honest in the activities one with another. And as He has given, "As ye do it unto the least of thy brethren, ye do it unto me."

Also He has given, as the Father's promise has been to Him and to man through those various channels of approach, "Ye abiding in me and I in the Father, ye may know that consciousness that I and the Father abide in thee." That is the manner in which the individual, the soul, may at *this* time become more and more aware of the Christ Con-sciousness, that manifested by and through the man Jesus, that is the promise and the sureness as shown in Him from the Father unto thee.

The way is simple. Yet those who would seek through the mysteries of nature, the mysteries of the manifestations of life in the earth, or those who would see rather the activities of their neighbors, friends, associates day by day, than listen to that which may be had through the still small voice from within, become in the position of being troubled and wondering—and then fearful; and then there come those periods when the sureness of self is lacking.

All things having force or power in the earth, in the heavens, in the sea, are given that power from Him; that those who seek may know Him the better. He hath not willed, He hath not destined that any soul should perish. In patience, in persistency, in consistency of thy manifes-tations of His love before and to and of thy fellow man, ye become aware that thy soul is a portion of the Creator, that it is the gift of the Father *to thee*. This is manifested in thine daily experience. That portion of thy body which is of the earth–earthy remains with the earth, but

that thou hast glorified, that thou hast used as a channel for the manifestations of His Spirit—of thy soul in communion with Him, *that* body
will be raised with Him in righteousness. That the physical body becomes ensnared, entangled in those things in the earth, through the
gratifying of those desires that are fleshly alone, those that are carnal, is
manifested by the dis-ease, the corruption, the turmoil, the strife that
arises within the experience of each soul in its *thoughtful* activities in the
earth.

The soul, then, must return—*will* return—to its Maker. It is a portion
of the Creative Force, which is energized into activity even in materiality, in the flesh. Yet it may, with thine own understanding and thine
own manifestations, come to be as a portion of that thou bringest in thy
love into thy fellow man, for thy Father-God, for thy activity to be *one*
with Him in those realms of activity and experience that ye *are* aware of
His presence, of His abiding love, of His abiding faith *in* thee motivating
thee in thy activities in every direction.

Then, just being kind, just being patient, just showing love for thy
fellow man; *that* is the manner in which an individual works *at* becoming aware of the consciousness of the Christ Spirit . . .

What are the rules, then? As has just been outlined, ye may become
aware of His presence abiding with thee. When ye manifest love, patience, hope, charity, tolerance, faith; these be the manners. Not in thine
own *self!* These as words, these as expressions, these as visualized *objects*
may be within thine self. But when ye as a soul, as an entity, as an
individual, make such manifest to those ye meet casually, to those that
ye contact day by day—in conversation, in example, in precept; these
the attributes of the Spirit—ye become aware of that Consciousness, of
that Christ Spirit, of that Christ Consciousness as He gave, "Ye abiding in
me and I in the Father, *we*—the Father, I will *come* and abide with thee."

When the Spirit of the Father, when the activities that the Christ—the
man—gave to the sons of men—are made manifest in thine own life day
by day, then ye become aware of His presence abiding in thee.

Know the Truth, for the truth is as He gave; the truth is He, and His
words. For He hath given, "Though the heavens and the earth may pass
away, *my* words, my promise, shall *not* pass away."

Let not, then, the cares of the world, the deceitfulness of riches, the pomp and glory of the earthly nature, or fame or even to be well-spoken of, hinder thee from *applying* in thy relationships with thy fellow man that thou *knowest* to be the manner in which ye may become aware of His presence.

That offenses must come is true. But woe to him that bringeth same to pass!

Then, be not idle in that ye know; rather let it be an *active, positive* influence in the experience of all. Let love be without dissimulation. Abhor that which is evil, cleave to that which is good.

In *this* way may *ye* know, may *ye* be aware of His presence within thee.

6

●

Jesus the Pattern as Spiritual Teacher

[Background: Nurse. Although this was a physical reading, the last question submitted by the woman was in regard to which spiritual teacher would be best for her.]

Reading 1299–1

(Q) Which spiritual teacher—Henry Victor Morgan, Emmet Fox, Helena Martin or Thelma Holden—would be best for me?

(A) Why not rather turn to Him that each of these would bring to thee—thyself? Begin with those promises He hath given. Read the 14th, 15th, 16th, 17th chapters of John. *Know* they are not to someone else but to thee! And why would you use other forces when He is so nigh?

For as He has given thee, "If it were not so I would have told you." And this means *you!* For the Father hath promised and has given us a body, that is a temple of the living soul, which is that temple in which ye should meet Him day by day.

For as the pattern was given even in the mount of old, when ye turn to Him, He will direct thee. Why, O Why, then, to any subordinate, when thy brother, thy Christ, thy Savior would speak with thee!

For He is not far away. For as has been given, do not say who will ascend into heaven to bring Him down, or who will come from over the seas to bring a message to me; for Lo, He is within thine own heart, thine own mind, and *there* ye may meet Him. For His messages have been, are, and ever will be for *thee*—not someone else! But "Put thy burdens on me, saith the Lord—Learn of me, for I am lowly even as thee—I am meek even as thee—I will give thee *rest* unto your soul, unto your mind!"

For the mind is both spiritual and physical in its attributes to the human body, and if ye feed thy body-mind upon worldly things, ye become worldly. If ye feed thy mind upon those things that are His, ye become His indeed.

And He stands at thy door and knocks, and bids that ye will let *Him* in! For He has promised, and His promises are sure!

[Background: From the 262 series, this particular reading addressed how the Study Group work could be presented to others, and the question was asked if they should study "the phenomena as manifest through Edgar Cayce?"]

Reading 262–100

Study that rather as manifested through the Christ. Study what happened when the water turned to wine, what happened when He took her by the hand and lifted her up, what happened when He walked to His disciples upon the sea, what happened when He called Lazarus, what happened in the garden when His disciples—even His closest friends—slept while He fought with self; what happened on the Cross when He commended His mother to John, what happened when He spoke to Mary Magdalene; what happened when He spoke to Thomas, to the other disciples; what happened when He arose, "Go ye into all the world and preach the gospel." What was that gospel? Not much that is being given so oft over and over. For He combined it all into one, "Thou shalt love the Lord thy God with all thy heart, thy mind, thy soul; thy neighbor as thyself." For this is the *whole* law the *whole* law. Hence ye would study to show thyself approved unto thy concept of thy God. What *is* thy God? Let each answer that within self. What *is* thy God? Where is He, what is He? Then ye may find yourselves lacking in much. How personal is He? Not as Moses painted a God of wrath; not as David painted a God that would fight thine enemies; but as the Christ—the

Father of love, of mercy, of justice. And man meets it in himself! How *can* it be then that ye do not understand God loves you, why do you suffer? It is mercy, it is justice to thy soul! For those things that are cares of the flesh and of the earth cannot inherit eternal life. Hence life alters, life changes in the experiences of individuals through their sojourns in the earth, and thus ye learn thy lessons, even as He; for though He were the Son, though ye are His sons and daughters, yet must *ye* learn obedience through the things that *ye* suffer.

[Background: Teacher (Ph.D.), Quaker, spiritualist. She was the head of the Department of Sociology at a college, a research worker, and a former missionary to India. This was her second life reading.]

Reading 2067–2

(Q) Considering my ideals, purposes and karmic pattern, as well as the conditions which I face at present, in what specific direction should I seek expression for my talents and abilities in order to render the greatest possible service?

(A) This is rather a compound question, for it presumes or presupposes as to ideals, as to purposes, and as to self's concept of karma.

What is karma? and what is the pattern?

He alone is each soul pattern. He *alone* is each soul pattern! *He* is thy *karma*, if ye put thy trust *wholly* in Him! See?

Not that every soul shall not give account for the deeds done in the body, and in the body meet them! but in each meeting, in *each* activity, let the pattern—(not in self, not in mind alone, but in Him)—be the guide.

As to the outlet, as to the manner of expression—to give as to this or that is merely giving opinions. For, all must be quickened—there must be the quickening of the spirit.

As we find indicated in the expression of thought, by or through writing is *one* manner, or one channel. Another is by the speaking, the becoming as a lecturer, an interpreter for groups of various sects or forms of activity—whether psychological groups, Theosophist groups, Sunday School groups of various denominations, or of whatever cult. For, the ideal is to set those aright! not by dogmatic activity but by reasoning—as He—with others.

When questioned as to political, economic or social order, what were

His answers? Did He condemn the man who was born blind? Did He condemn the woman taken in adultery? Did He condemn the man that was healed of palsy or of leprosy? Did He condemn any? Rather did He point out that in *Him* each meets that karmic condition found in self, and that the pattern is in Him; doing good, being kind, being patient, being loving in *every* experience of man's activity.

Do thou likewise . . .

(Q) *What is the purpose of my reincarnating at this time?*

(A) That He may be manifested in thee.

[Background: Insurance agent, Protestant. This was a follow-up life reading in which he inquired whether it was possible to use meditation to answer any question.]

Reading 2533–4

(Q) *Outline additional comprehensive instructions that will enable this entity to meditate on any problem that may arise and get the solution.*

(A) As has been indicated so oft for others, as well as for this entity— ye as an individual are made in the image of the Creator. Ye are, as an individual, remembered by Him—which is demonstrated in thy awareness of thy ability, thy consciousness in the present of being alive and conscious of the faults and the failures of thy fellow man about you, and of thine own shortcomings in meeting or fulfilling all of thine own ideals as to the relationship an individual soul–entity should bear to the Creative Forces or God.

Yet ye realize the possibilities, the opportunities that lie latent within. For, as was given of old—Say not as to who will descend from heaven that ye may have a message, for Lo, it is in thine own heart. For, thy body is indeed the temple of the living God. There He—as all knowledge, all undertakings, all wisdom, all understanding—may commune with thee, if ye but give that opportunity, that force an opportunity to open thine heart, thine mind, thy understanding, to His presence.

Ye believe, and ye know, and ye understand, that His Son, thy Brother, entered into the flesh that ye might have not only that promise of old that man has gotten so far from, but that ye might today have an advocate with the Father; that ye might know not only that thine own angel

of thyself, what thou hast been, stands ever as the evidence of thy consciousness, thy awareness, thy presence in the throne of the Father, but
that thy Brother, thy Representative, thy Friend, stands ever ready to
intercede for thee. And, as He hath given, He stands continually at the
door of thy consciousness, of thy heart. If ye will open, He will enter.

How do ye open? By attuning, turning thy thought, thy purpose, thy
desire to be at an at-onement with Him. The atonement has been offered. Thus ye have that assurance that as ye seek His face He will come
and abide.

Thus, as ye seek for any purpose—worthy or unworthy—these will be
made known to thee, and the course thou shouldst pursue. In this, even
as He:

Not my will, Lord, but Thine be done in me, through me, day by day. May I ever
be the channel that may bring to my fellow man that awareness of Thy love—by the
manner in which I, myself, treat my fellow man day by day; knowing, in my own
heart and mind, that inasmuch as or in the manner I treat my brother, here, I am
treating my brother who stands in my stead before Thy throne.

**[Background: College sophomore. This was a life reading in which she
inquired about the nature of her life's work.]**

Reading 1981-1

Remember, only in Christ, Jesus, do extremes meet. And in thy activity through each experience, ask self oft, "What would Jesus have me
do?" For He faileth not those who seek.

And thus comes those experiences in the activity in every phase of
thy experience . . .

Know that it is not by chance that one enters a material experience;
rather the combination of minds as would create the channel to be
offered for the expression of a soul, and the soul seeks same because of
those desires of the two making one—thus bringing the opportunity.

Thus, those environs may change; and those activities of individuals
may be changed by those influences that appear to be without the scope
or cope of man's activity. All of these are oft visioned by the soul before
it enters, and all of these are at times met in tempering the soul.

For, remember, He hath not willed that any soul should perish, but hath with each temptation, with each experience offered a channel, a choice whereby the soul is enlarged, is shown that the choice brings it nearer, nearer yet, to that purpose for which expression is given of same in the material world; even as He, the way, the life, the truth, came into life in materiality that we, through Him might have the advocate with the Father, and thus in Him find the answer to every problem in material experience.

[Background: Housewife, Protestant. This was a life reading.]

Reading 1504-1

For as one soweth, so one reaps; else the very Divine would be mocked among the children of men.

Hence it is not by works alone but by grace and mercy, and the gift of the Father, that man comes to know His relationships with the things that are, that have been, and that may be in the experience of each soul in its journey through those environs, those phases of experience that bring the more and more awareness of the divine love as may be expressed, manifested in a *material* world—as well as in the mental and the spiritual.

For indeed it is given to man to know. Even as His Prayer, "Thy will be done in the earth as it is in heaven" may become the very life blood of every soul if it will but harken to that still small voice within that answers to thy own good conscience as to whether or not ye be manifesting the God-like life; as to whether ye *are* the sons and daughters of God or as to whether ye be making manifest thy own desires, thy own indulgences, thy own self . . .

For hope and faith are living—*living*—things! Thus hope springs anew with the growth and the knowledge and the understanding of the light on the way, and that life indeed is an eternal expression of the love of the Father; and that as it gives the expression through the individuality of each and every soul as it comes in material manifestation by the weaknesses, we find the strength in the Lord—and in the glories ever in His beauteous purpose with each soul; that purpose that ye might be the companions, one with Him.

Then indeed may there be a glimpse of the love the Father hath shown to the children of men, through the very gift of Him, thy Brother, the Christ; that we may walk circumspectly one with another; and thus give, show forth, *His* activity in the earth till we be made as one with Him, in the glories that were His and that are as He has given for us. For we be joint heirs, as one with Him; not strangers, not aliens but joint heirs with the Christ to the kingdom of the Father—that is, that was, that ever shall be—even before the foundations of the earth were laid.

Hence we find to keep, to hold to those things as He gave in the beginning, "Subdue ye the earth—make ye then the laws thereof thy servants, not thy enemies"—this is saying only "Sin not; for ye that know sin and have fallen short must meet these in thyself." And only as He hath shown the way. Though He were in the world, He was not of the world; yet subject to the laws thereof, of materiality.

For His heart ached, yea His body was sore and weary; yea His body bled not only from the nail prints in His hands and feet but from the spear thrust into the heart of hearts! For the blood as of the perfect man was shed, not by reason of Himself but that there might be made an offering once for all; that then *ye* may know, ye in thine own self are not a burden to any.

For with thy mind, thy heart, ye may give much, much the more to those about thee in their ministry to thy physical weaknesses; that the very glory of Him may be manifested in their lives.

For if we do good only to those that would do good to us, what praise, what profit is there in same? For it was the unjustness of His trial, the persecutions of His body, that made the way for mankind, ye His brethren, ye thy own self, to *have* and know the way that leads to "That peace I leave with thee; not as the world knoweth peace, but my peace I give," in that:

Though ye be hindered, though ye be misunderstood, yea though ye be persecuted for those things that are not even thine own faults—how much greater is the manifestation of His glory for that which was a shortcoming in thee to be made right in ministering good unto others through the love He hath shown to thee? . . .

Father-Mother God, here am I—thy handmaid! Weak, unworthy though I may be, I come seeking divine light, divine guidance; believing Thou hearest the prayers of those that would know Thy face! Lead thou, O Lord, the way!

Let my body, my mind, be in this experience a manifestation of the love Thou hast promised to the children of men.

Then use my abilities, my purposes, my desires, in the way Thou seest, O lord, these should go.

[Background: This was among a series of readings given on the topic of Jesus. This particular reading was given to the first Study Group.]

Reading 5749-4

As He, the Christ, is in His glory that was ordained of the Father, He may be approached by those who in sincerity and earnestness seek to know Him—and to be guided by Him. As He has given, by faith all things are made possible through belief in His name.

Believest thou? Then let thine activities bespeak that thou wouldst have, in spirit, in truth.

Seek, then, each in your own way and manner, to magnify that you, as souls, as beings, would make manifest of His love, in the way He will show thee day by day.

As He came into the world, as man knows the world, then He became as man; yet in the spirit world He seeks to make manifest that sought by those who do His biddings.

For, as He gave, "If ye love me, keep my commandments. These are not new, and are not grievous, that ye love one another—even as the Father loveth me."

(Q) [993]: Please explain why during meditation last Monday noon I had the longing to seek more knowledge of, and a reading on, Jesus the Christ.

(A) The inner self approached nearer the attunement of the consciousness of the Christ presence.

The Christ Consciousness is a universal consciousness of the Father Spirit. The Jesus consciousness is that man builds as body worship.

In the Christ Consciousness, then, there is the oneness of self, self's desires, self's abilities, made in at-onement with the forces that may bring to pass that which is sought by an individual entity or soul. Hence at that particular period self was in accord. Hence the physical consciousness had the desire to make it an experience of the whole consciousness of self.

Seek this the more often. He will speak with thee, for His promises
are true—every one of them.

*(Q) [560]: Please explain: While meditating I had the realization of the forces
within and the forces without being the one and the same force. Then as if someone
said: "Why not look to the within?" When I turned to the within, I received a realization of the Christ which seemed to take form in body.*

(A) In this the body–consciousness experienced much that "I, even
John, experienced when I looked behind me from the cave and saw that
the without and within are *one,*" [John 11:38? John's witnessing the healing of Lazarus?] when the desires of the heart make each atom of the
physical body vibrate with the consciousness of, the belief and the faith
and the presence of, the Christ life, the Christ Consciousness.

Life is an essence of the Father. The Christ, taking up the life of the
man Jesus, becomes life in glory; and may be glorified in each atom of
a physical body that attunes self to the consciousness and the *will* of the
Christ Spirit.

*(Q) [69]: Is the Celestial Sphere a definite place in the Universe or is it a state of
mind?*

(A) When an entity, a soul, passes into any sphere, with that it has
builded in its celestial body, it must occupy—to a finite mind—space,
place, time. Hence, to a finite mind, a body can only be in a place, a
position. An attitude, sure—for that of a onement with, or attunement
with, the Whole.

For, God is love; hence occupies a space, place, condition, and *is* the
Force that permeates all activity.

So, Christ is the ruling force in the world that man, in his finite mind—
the material body, must draw to self of that sphere of which the entity,
the soul, is a part, of whatever period of experience, to be conscious of
an existence in that particular sphere or plane.

*(Q) Is Jesus the Christ on any particular sphere or is He manifesting on the earth
plane in another body?*

(A) As just given, all power in heaven, in earth, is given to Him who
overcame. Hence He is of Himself in space, in the force that impels
through faith, through belief, in the individual entity. As a Spirit Entity.
Hence not in a body in the earth, but may come at will to him who *wills*
to be one with, and acts in love to make same possible.

For, He shall come as ye have seen Him go, in the *body* He occupied in Galilee. The body that He formed, that was crucified on the cross, that rose from the tomb, that walked by the sea, that appeared to Simon, that appeared to Philip . . .

(Q) [379]: *How may I raise my vibrations so as to contact the Christ?*

(A) Making the will, the desire of the heart, one with His, believing in faith, in patience, all becomes possible in Him, through Him to the Father; for He gave it as it is. Believest thou?

Then, "according to thy faith be it done in thee".

7

●

Special Readings on Jesus as the Pattern

[Background: This was a special reading given to Thomas Sugrue when he was compiling the "Philosophy" chapter of Cayce's biography *There Is a River*.]

Reading 5749–14

HLC: You will have before you the enquiring mind of the entity, Thomas Sugrue, present in this room, and certain of the problems which confront him in composing the manuscript of *There Is a River*.

The entity is now ready to describe the philosophical concepts which have been given through this source, and wishes to parallel and align them with known religious tenets, especially those of Christian theology.

The entity does not wish to set forth a system of thought, nor imply that all questions of a philosophical nature can be answered through this source—the limitations of the finite mind prevent this.

But the entity wishes to answer those questions which will naturally arise in the mind of the reader, and many of the questions which are being asked by all people in the world today.

Therefore the entity presents certain problems and questions, which you will answer as befits the entity's understanding and the task of interpretation before him.

EC: Yes, we have the enquiring mind, Thomas Sugrue, and those problems, those questions that arise in the mind of the entity at this period. Ready for questions.

(Q) The first problem concerns the reason for creation. Should this be given as God's desire to experience Himself, God's desire for companionship, God's desire for expression, or in some other way?

(A) God's desire for companionship and expression.

(Q) The second problem concerns that which is variously called evil, darkness, negation, sin. Should it be said that this condition existed as a necessary element of creation, and the soul, given free will, found itself with the power to indulge in it, or lose itself in it? Or should it be said that this is a condition created by the activity of the soul itself? Should it be described, in either case, as a state of consciousness, a gradual lack of awareness of self and self's relation to God?

(A) It is the free will and its losing itself in its relationship to God.

(Q) The third problem has to do with the fall of man. Should this be described as something which was inevitable in the destiny of souls, or something which God did not desire, but which He did not prevent once He had given free will? The problem here is to reconcile the omniscience of God and His knowledge of all things with the free will of the soul and the soul's fall from grace.

(A) He did not prevent, once having given free will. For, He made the individual entities or souls in the beginning. For, the beginnings of sin, of course, were in seeking expression of themselves outside of the plan or the way in which God had expressed same. Thus it was the individual, see?

Having given free will, then—though having the foreknowledge, though being omnipotent and omnipresent—it is only when the soul that is a portion of God *chooses* that God knows the end thereof.

(Q) The fourth problem concerns man's tenancy on earth. Was it originally intended that souls remain out of earthly forms, and were the races originated as a necessity resulting from error?

(A) The earth and its manifestations were only the expression of God and not necessarily as a place of tenancy for the souls of men, until man was created—to meet the needs of existing conditions.

(Q) The fifth problem concerns an explanation of the Life Readings. From a study of these it seems that there is a trend downward, from early incarnations, toward greater earthliness and less mentality. Then there is a swing upward, accompanied by

suffering, patience, and understanding. Is this the normal pattern, which results in virtue and oneness with God obtained by free will and mind?

(A) This is correct. It is the pattern as it is set in Him.

(Q) The sixth problem concerns interplanetary and inter-system dwelling, between earthly lives. It was given through this source that the entity Edgar Cayce, after the experience as Uhjltd, went to the system of Arcturus, and then returned to earth. Does this indicate a usual or an unusual step in soul evolution?

(A) As indicated, or as has been indicated in other sources besides this as respecting this very problem—Arcturus is that which may be called the center of this universe, through which individuals pass and at which period there comes the choice of the individual as to whether it is to return to complete there—that is, in this planetary system, our sun, the earth sun and its planetary system—or to pass on to others. This was an unusual step, and yet a usual one.

(Q) The seventh problem concerns implications from the sixth problem. Is it necessary to finish the solar system cycle before going to other systems?

(A) Necessary to finish the solar cycle.

(Q) Can oneness be attained—or the finish of evolution reached—on any system, or must it be in a particular one?

(A) Depending upon what system the entity has entered, to be sure. It may be completed in any of the many systems.

(Q) Must the solar cycle be finished on earth, or can it be completed on another planet, or does each planet have a cycle of its own which must be finished?

(A) If it is begun on the earth it must be finished on the earth. The solar system of which the earth is a part is only a portion of the whole. For, as indicated in the number of planets about the earth, they are of one and the same—and they are relative one to another. It is the cycle of the whole system that is finished, see?

(Q) The eighth problem concerns the pattern made by parents at conception. Should it be said that this pattern attracts a certain soul because it approximates conditions which that soul wishes to work with?

(A) It approximates conditions. It does not set. For, the individual entity or soul, given the opportunity, has its own free will to work in or out of those problems as presented by that very union. Yet the very union, of course, attracts or brings a channel or an opportunity for the expression of an individual entity.

(Q) Does the incoming soul take on of necessity some of the parents' karma?

(A) Because of its relative relationship to same, yes. Otherwise, no.

(Q) Does the soul itself have an earthly pattern which fits back into the one created by the parents?

(A) Just as indicated, it is relative—as one related to another; and because of the union of activities they are brought in the pattern. For in such there is the explanation of universal or divine laws, which are ever one and the same; as indicated in the expression that God moved within Himself and then He didn't change, though did bring to Himself that of His own being made crucified even in the flesh.

(Q) Are there several patterns which a soul might take on, depending on what phase of development it wished to work upon—i.e., could a soul choose to be one of several personalities, any of which would fit its individuality?

(A) Correct.

(Q) Is the average fulfillment of the soul's expectation more or less than fifty percent?

(A) It's a continuous advancement, so it is more than fifty percent.

(Q) Are hereditary, environment and will equal factors in aiding or retarding the entity's development?

(A) Will is the greater factor, for it may overcome any or all of the others; provided that will is made one with the pattern, see? For, no influence of heredity, environment or what not, surpasses the will; else why would there have been that pattern shown in which the individual soul, no matter how far astray it may have gone, may enter with Him into the holy of holies?

(Q) The ninth problem concerns the proper symbols, or similes, for the Master, the Christ. Should Jesus be described as the soul who first went through the cycle of earthly lives to attain perfection, including perfection in the planetary lives also?

(A) He should be. This is as the man, see?

(Q) Should this be described as a voluntary mission One Who was already perfected and returned to God, having accomplished His Oneness in other planes and systems?

(A) Correct.

(Q) Should the Christ Consciousness be described as the awareness within each soul, imprinted in pattern on the mind and waiting to be awakened by the will, of the soul's oneness with God?

(A) Correct. That's the idea exactly!

(Q) *Please list the names of the incarnations of the Christ, and of Jesus, indicating where the development of the man Jesus began.*

(A) First, in the beginning, of course; and then as Enoch, Melchizedek, in the perfection. Then in the earth of Joseph, Joshua, Jeshua, Jesus.

(Q) *The tenth problem concerns the factors of soul evolution. Should mind, the builder, be described as the last development because it should not unfold until it has a firm foundation of emotional virtues?*

(A) This might be answered Yes and No, both. But if it is presented in that there is kept, willfully, see, that desire to be in the at–onement, then it is necessary for that attainment before it recognizes mind as the way.

(Q) *The eleventh problem concerns a parallel with Christianity. Is Gnosticism the closest type of Christianity to that which is given through this source?*

(A) This is a parallel, and was the commonly accepted one until there began to be set rules in which there were the attempts to take short cuts. And there are none in Christianity!

(Q) *What action of the early church, or council, can be mentioned as that which ruled reincarnation from Christian theology?*

(A) Just as indicated—the attempts of individuals to accept or take advantage of, because of this knowledge, see?

(Q) *Do souls become entangled in other systems as they did in this system?*

(A) In other systems that represent the same as the earth does in this system, yes.

(Q) *Is there any other advice which may be given to this entity at this time in the preparation of these chapters?*

(A) Hold fast to that ideal, and using Him ever as the Ideal. And hold up that *necessity* for each to meet the same problems. And *do not* attempt to shed or to surpass or go around the Cross. *This* is that upon which each and every soul *must* look and know it is to be borne in self *with* Him.

We are through for the present.

[Background: Stockbroker, Jewish. Mr. (900) received hundreds of readings from Edgar Cayce in a span of six years. He had a keen interest in dreams and metaphysical and spiritual subjects.]

Reading 900-10

(Q) As created by God in the first, are souls perfect, and if so, why any need of development?

(A) In this we find only the answer in this: The evolution of life as may be understood by the finite mind. In the first cause, or principle, all is perfect. In the creation of soul, we find the portion may become a living soul and equal with the Creator. To reach that position, when separated, must pass through all stages of development, that it may be one with the Creator. As we have is this:

Man. In the beginning, we find the spirit existent in all living force. When such force becomes inanimate in finite forces [it is] called dead; not necessarily losing its usefulness, either to Creator, or created, in material world. In that of creation of man, we find all the elements in a living, moving, world, or an element in itself; yet without that experience as of a first cause, yet endowed with all the various modifications of elements or forces manifested in each. For first there is the spirit, then soul (man we are speaking of), then mind with its various modifications and with its various incentives, with its various ramifications, if you please, and the will the balance in the force that may make all or lose all.

In the developing, then, that the man may be one with the Father, necessary that the soul pass, with its companion the will, through all the various stages of development, until the will is lost in Him and he becomes one with the Father.

In the illustration of this, we find in the man as called Jesus. In this: This man, as man, makes the will the will of the Father, then becoming one with the Father and the model for man . . .

(Q) Name the planets in order of the soul's development and give the principal influence of each.

(A) These have been given. Their influences, their developments may be changed from time to time, according to the individual's will forces, speaking from human viewpoint. This we find again illustrated in this:

In this man called Jesus we find at a One-ness with the Father, the Creator, passing through all the various stages of development. In mental perfect, in wrath perfect, in flesh made perfect, in love become perfect, in death become perfect, in psychic become perfect, in mystic become perfect, in consciousness become perfect, in the greater ruling forces becoming perfect, and is as the model, and through the compliance with such laws made perfect, destiny, the pre–destined, the forethought, the will, made perfect. The condition made perfect, and is an ensample for man, and only as a man, for He lived only as man. He died as man.

[Background: From the 262 series, this particular reading came in response to the Study Group asking about the birth of Jesus and the celebration of Christmas.]

Reading 262–103

GC: You will have before you the members of the Norfolk Study Group #1 who have gathered here seeking a reading which will give them a better understanding and deeper appreciation of the birth of Jesus, the Christ, which will be celebrated this week as Christmas 1936.

EC: Yes, we have the group as gathered here and their desires and their seeking as a group, as individuals.

In giving to these, then, that seek to know more of that circumstance, those conditions as surrounded that ye call the first Christmas: Do not confuse thyselves. While to you it may be a first Christmas, if it were the first then there would be a last; and ye would not worship, ye would not hold to that which passeth.

For time never was when there was not a Christ and not a Christ mass.

But in giving that interpretation of what this Season means—that birth of Jesus as became the Christ—to this world: In giving the circumstance, much has been recorded as respecting this by the writers of the Gospel, especially by Luke; but little perfect concept may be gathered except ye as individuals seek to experience what such an advent meant or means to thy life as an individual.

For knowledge of a thing or a condition and the wisdom that is presented in that happening are two different things. What ye hear ye may believe, but ye will rarely act as if ye believed it unless ye have experienced and do experience that "God so loved the world as to give His Son" to enter into flesh, that flesh, that man, might know there *is* an advocate with the Father; and that—as ye in thy material experience see—Life coming from out of nowhere to enter into materiality, to become a *living* expression of those promptings of the heart.

That has been the experience of that *soul* in its varied spheres of consciousness, to give such an expression. That is the purpose for which it has entered—to give the more perfect concept of the relationships of man to the Creator.

Such we find as that happening in Bethlehem of Judea ages and years ago, when that channel had so dedicated itself to the service of her Maker as to become *Mother*, wherein the whole world is shown that this must come to pass in the experience of those who would make themselves channels through which the Holy Spirit of God may manifest; that the world may know that He, God the Father, keepeth His promises with the children of men!

And the hour approaches when nature is to be fulfilled in the natural courses in the experience of the Mother, and His Star has appeared— and the angels' choir, and the voices of those that give the *great message!*

Who heard these, my children? Those that were seeking for the satisfying of their own desires or for the laudation of their own personality? Rather those close to *nature*, to the hours of meditation and prayer, and those that had given expression, "No room in the Inn!" For no inn, no room, could contain that as was being given in a manifested form!

For He came unto His own. For there was nothing made that was made to which He had not given life, to whom He had not given, "Be ye fruitful, multiply—" in *thyself; in thyself* may there be the propagation of thine own specie, of thine own self!

Only then to those that sought could such a message come, or could there be heard the songs of the angels, or that music of the spheres that sang, *"Peace on earth—good will to men!"*

For this, then, is in *every* birth—the possibilities, the glories, the actuating of that influence of that entrance again of god–man into the earth that man might know the way.

Thus this comes at this time to bring to the hearts and minds of those of that Glad period the fact that not only 1900 years ago but *today*, He may be born into thine own consciousness, thine own understanding; He comes unto His own!

Art thou His? Have ye claimed Him? Have ye put on the Christ, even as was and is exemplified in that life, that birth, that death of Jesus, the Christ?

For He is thy Elder Brother, He *is* the babe in thy heart, in thy life; to be then even now—as then—nourished in the heart, in body, in mind. And indeed do His words become more and more then of meaning, "As ye do it unto the least of these, thy brethren, ye do it unto me!"

For as ye behold the face of thy friend, of thy neighbor, of thy foe, yea thine enemy, ye behold the image of thy Savior.

For ye are all His, bought not only with the birth of the God-Child into flesh but with the death—that ye might know that He, thy Brother, thy Savior, thy Christ, has been and is the Way to the Father in this material plane.

For as He chose to enter, so *ye* have entered. As He chose to live, so may ye live. As He chose to give of Himself that there might be a greater understanding, a greater knowledge; yea, the showing forth of the wisdom of God that God *is* love, poured forth upon the children of men in this experience.

And as these changes come and as ye make known that as has been the raising of that consciousness of His Presence in *thine* experience, by thy dealings with, by thy conversation with, by thy life with thy fellow man, so may ye hasten the day when *He, Christ,* may come into thine own heart, unto His *own* peoples, to reign; yes, in the hearts and lives!

Then indeed should each of you at this Glad Season make the hearts of others Merry by thine own happiness in the birth, the life, the death of thy Jesus, thy Christ!

Know this had no beginning in the 1900 years ago, but again and Again and *again!* And it may be today, He may be born into thy consciousness; not as a physical birth—but each moment that a physical birth is experienced in the earth is an *opportunity* for the Christ-entrance again!

Then what are ye doing about it in thy daily life, thy daily conversation? For not by might nor in power, but in the still small voice that speaks within, ye may know as He hath given so oft—"Peace—it is I! Be not afraid, it is I," thy Savior, thy Christ; yea, *thyself* meeting that *babe* in thine own inner self that may grow even as He to be a channel of blessings to others!

For as ye do it unto others ye do it unto Him.

May the Peace, the Joy of His Consciousness, His Presence, His Joy be thine this day; yea, all thy days in the earth! For He is nigh unto thee, He is in thy midst!

Praise ye the Lord that gave, then, His Son; that ye might know Him! We are through.

[Background: This was a voluntary reading that came at the end of check-physical reading (1315-3), after the suggestion was given three times for Edgar Cayce to wake up.]

Reading 5749-1

EC: The Lord's Supper—here with the Master—see what they had for supper—boiled fish, rice, with leeks, wine, and loaf. One of the pitchers in which it was served was broken—the handle was broken, as was the lip to same.

The whole robe of the Master was not white, but pearl gray—all combined into one—the gift of Nicodemus to the Lord.

The better looking of the twelve, of course, was Judas, while the younger was John—oval face, dark hair, smooth face—only one with the short hair. Peter, the rough and ready—always that of very short beard, rough, and not altogether clean; while Andrew's is just the opposite—very sparse, but inclined to be long more on the side and under the chin—long on the upper lip—his robe was always near gray or black, while his clouts or breeches were striped; while those of Philip and Bartholomew were red and brown.

The Master's hair is 'most red, inclined to be curly in portions, yet not feminine or weak—*strong*, with heavy piercing eyes that are blue or steel-gray.

His weight would be at least a hundred and seventy pounds. Long tapering fingers, nails well kept. Long nail, though, on the left little finger.

Merry—even in the hour of trial. Joke—even in the moment of betrayal.

The sack is empty. Judas departs.

The last is given of the wine and loaf, with which He gives the emblems that should be so dear to every follower of Him. Lays aside His robe, which is all of one piece—girds the towel about His waist, which is dressed with linen that is blue and white. Rolls back the folds, kneels first before John, James, then to Peter—who refuses.

Then the dissertation as to "He that would be the greatest would be servant of all."

The basin is taken as without handle, and is made of wood. The water is from the gherkins [gourds], that are in the wide-mouth Shibboleths [streams? Judges 12:6], that stand in the house of John's father, Zebedee.

And now comes "It is finished."

They sing the ninety-first Psalm—"He that dwelleth in the secret place of the Most High shall abide under the shadow of the Almighty. I will say of the Lord, He is my refuge and my fortress: my God; in Him will I trust."

He is the musician as well, for He uses the harp.

They leave for the garden.

[Background: This reading was requested by Edgar Cayce for background information in regard to a talk he was going to give on the Second Coming.]

Reading 5749-5

Then, He has come in all ages when it has been necessary for the understanding to be centered in a *new* application of the same thought, "God *is* Spirit and seeks such to worship him in spirit and in truth!"

Then, as there is prepared the way by those that have made and do make the channels for the entering in, there may come into the earth those influences that will save, regenerate, resuscitate, *hold*—if you please—the earth in its continued activity toward the proper understanding and proper relationships to that which is the making for the closer relationships to that which is in Him *alone*. Ye have seen it in Adam; ye have heard it in Enoch, ye have had it made known in Melchizedek; Joshua, Joseph, David, and those that made the preparation then for him called Jesus. [GD's note: Essenes, School of Prophets started by Elijah. See Malachi 3 and 4] Ye have seen His Spirit in the leaders in all realms of activity, whether in the isles of the sea, the wilderness, the mountain, or in the various activities of every race, every color, every activity of that which has produced and does produce contention in the minds and hearts of those that dwell in the flesh.

For, what must be obliterated? Hate, prejudice, selfishness, backbiting, unkindness, anger, passion, and those things of the mire that are created in the activities of the sons of men.

Then again He may come in body to claim His own. Is He abroad today in the earth? Yea, in those that cry unto Him from every corner; for He, the Father, hath not suffered His soul to see corruption; neither hath it taken hold on those things that make the soul afraid. For, He *is* the Son of Light, of God, and is holy before Him. And He comes again in the hearts and souls and minds of those that seek to know His ways.

These be hard to be understood by those in the flesh, where prejudice, avarice, vice of all natures holds sway in the flesh; yet those that call on Him will not go empty handed—even as thou, in thine ignorance, in thine zealousness that has at times eaten thee up. Yet *here* ye may hear the golden sceptre ring—ring—in the hearts of those that seek His face. Ye, too, may minister in those days when He will come in the flesh, in the earth, to call His own by name.

We are through.

A.R.E. PRESS

The A.R.E. Press publishes books, videos, audiotapes, CDs, and DVDs meant to improve the quality of our readers' lives—personally, professionally, and spiritually. We hope our products support your endeavors to realize your career potential, to enhance your relationships, to improve your health, and to encourage you to make the changes necessary to live a loving, joyful, and fulfilling life.

For more information or to receive a free catalog, call:

800–333–4499

Or write:

> A.R.E. Press
> 215 67th Street
> Virginia Beach, VA 23451-2061

ARE PRESS.COM

BAAR PRODUCTS

A.R.E.'s Official Worldwide Exclusive Supplier of Edgar Cayce Health Care Products

Baar Products, Inc., is the official worldwide exclusive supplier of Edgar Cayce health care products. Baar offers a collection of natural products and remedies drawn from the work of Edgar Cayce, considered by many to be the father of modern holistic medicine.

For a complete listing of Cayce-related products, call:

800–269–2502

Or write:

> Baar Products, Inc.
> P.O. Box 60
> Downingtown, PA 19335 U.S.A.
>
> Customer Service and International: 610-873-4591
> Fax: 610-873-7945
> Web Site: www.baar.com   E-mail: cayce@baar.com

EDGAR CAYCE'S A.R.E.

What Is A.R.E.?

The Association for Research and Enlightenment, Inc., (A.R.E.©) was founded in 1931 to research and make available information on psychic development, dreams, holistic health, meditation, and life after death. As an open–membership research organization, the A.R.E. continues to study and publish such information, to initiate research, and to promote conferences, distance learning, and regional events. Edgar Cayce, the most documented psychic of our time, was the moving force in the establishment of A.R.E.

Who Was Edgar Cayce?

Edgar Cayce (1877–1945) was born on a farm near Hopkinsville, Ky. He was an average individual in most respects. Yet, throughout his life, he manifested one of the most remarkable psychic talents of all time. As a young man, he found that he was able to enter into a self–induced trance state, which enabled him to place his mind in contact with an unlimited source of information. While asleep, he could answer questions or give accurate discourses on any topic. These discourses, more than 14,000 in number, were transcribed as he spoke and are called "readings."

Given the name and location of an individual anywhere in the world, he could correctly describe a person's condition and outline a regimen of treatment. The consistent accuracy of his diagnoses and the effectiveness of the treatments he prescribed made him a medical phenomenon, and he came to be called the "father of holistic medicine."

Eventually, the scope of Cayce's readings expanded to include such subjects as world religions, philosophy, psychology, parapsychology, dreams, history, the missing years of Jesus, ancient civilizations, soul growth, psychic development, prophecy, and reincarnation.

A.R.E. Membership

People from all walks of life have discovered meaningful and life–transforming insights through membership in A.R.E. To learn more about Edgar Cayce's A.R.E. and how membership in the A.R.E. can enhance your life, visit our Web site at EdgarCayce.org, or call us toll–free at 800–333–4499.

Edgar Cayce's A.R.E.
215 67th Street
Virginia Beach, VA 23451–2061

EDGARCAYCE.ORG